Collingwood's Northumbrians

Old and Valuable Officers

Tony Barrow

© Tony Barrow

ISBN 978 1 901888 60 7

First published 2010

Cover Design by Tim Murphy Creative Solutions

With thanks to Tyne & Wear Archives and Museums for endorsing this publication.

Published in Great Britain by
Business Education Publishers
e-volve Business Centre
Cygnet Way
Rainton Bridge Business Park
Tyne and Wear
DH4 5QY

Tel: 0191 3055165
Fax: 0191 3055504

British Cataloguing-in-Publications Data
A catalogue record for this book is available from the British Library

Printed in Great Britain by Ashford Colour Press Ltd.

Dedicated to the memory of Tony Lea (1934-2008)

Master Mariner and Lt-Cdr RNR

An officer and a gentleman

Contents

Illustrations

Cover

The Battle of the Saintes, 1782
National Maritime Museum, London

Part One

Admiral Robert Roddam (1719-1808)
National Maritime Museum, London

Roddam Hall
Author's collection with permission of Lord & Lady Vinson

Roddam Family Mausoleum at Ilderton
Author's collection

Warships off Portsmouth Harbour
Tyne & Wear Archives and Museums

Dreadnought [104] lying off Greenwich
National Maritime Museum, London

Collingwood's Captain: Edward Rotheram
National Maritime Museum, London

The Day After Trafalgar
National Maritime Museum, London

Rotheram's grave at Bildeston in Suffolk
Author's collection

The Battle of the Saintes
National Maritime Museum, London

Extract from the journal of the *Monarch*, April 1782

Admiral Lord Collingwood
Tyne & Wear Archives and Museums

Part Two

Preface

The idea for this book grew from research for a previous volume *Trafalgar Geordies* published in 2005. That book explored the experience of seamen from North East England who fought the guns of the British fleet at the Battle of Trafalgar and was written as a contribution to the bicentenary celebrations, and the Year of the Sea. This book is published to coincide with another bicentenary; Collingwood's own death on board his flagship *Ville de Paris* [110]* in March 1810. It gives a focus to the lives and careers of some of the Northumbrian naval officers who came together under Collingwood's command in the years surrounding Trafalgar. Their careers were, perhaps, more typical than Collingwood's although their character and experience was very different. During a naval career lasting almost half a century Collingwood spent 42 years at sea, fought at three of the major naval battles of the French Wars and, after Trafalgar, as Commander-in-Chief Mediterranean Fleet, directed the naval and diplomatic efforts to frustrate the genius of Napoleon. Only his fellow Northumbrian and long-time patron, Admiral Robert Roddam, boasted a longer active career.

But few of the thousands of officers who served in the Georgian navy during the French Wars rose to command fleets as they did. For the generality of naval officers their experience of active service was usually shorter although often just as fascinating. Collectively, Collingwood's Northumbrians participated in many of the major naval events of that era.

---

*The figure in brackets refers to the number of guns the ship carried.

His lieutenant, William Landless was captured at Yorktown in 1781, fought at the Battle of the Saintes the following year and witnessed the Mutiny at the Nore in 1797. His flag-captain, Edward Rotheram, also fought at that battle in 1782 as well as the Glorious First of June in 1794. His young midshipmen, Granville Thompson and George Castle, distinguished themselves in numerous boat attacks and 'cutting out' expeditions. All of them fought at Trafalgar. Their stories help to illuminate a Northumbrian naval tradition and provide a context in which Admiral Collingwood's life and achievements might be better appreciated during the public events associated with the bicentenary of his death.

It only remains for me to acknowledge the help and support I have received from numerous individuals over the past four years. In particular, Dr. Steven Smith, whose diligence and willingness to take on, often at short notice, some concentrated research amongst the Admiralty collections at the National Archives, has been indispensible. Professor Norman McCord has, as ever, been generous with his advice, especially in pointing me towards the potential of several primary source collections in the region. Professor McCord's willingness to share his extensive knowledge of the history of North East England, read through draft chapters of the book, discuss amendments and save me from error, has been crucial to the success of the project. It goes without saying that any surviving errors in the text are entirely my responsibility. Of the many other individuals who have assisted, advised and encouraged during the research phases, a number of the usual suspects deserve my thanks. Adrian Osler for his ability to quarry fascinating gems from unusual sources; Bill Purdue whose encyclopaedic knowledge and published work on Northumberland families helped to provide a context for Collingwood's naval career; Ian Whitehead, Curator of Maritime Collections at Newcastle Discovery, has encouraged this project since its inception and facilitated my access to a number of images from fine art collections in the region. Archivists, Carol Scott, Keith Gilroy and Linda Bankier, together with my former colleague, Dr. Liz O'Donnell, at Northumberland Record Office, handled my requests for obscure documents with patience and professionalism. Val Glass, Joan Wright, David Morrison and Philippa Craig of Belford Local History Society, together with Tony and Iris Oates of Easington Farm, will recognise their particular contributions to the content of Chapter 4 and I take this opportunity to thank them for it. I am also grateful for the hospitality extended to me by Lord Vinson, the current owner of Roddam Hall and its surrounding estate, who kindly allowed me into his home to view some of the surviving artefacts from Admiral Roddam's time. My visit was made more memorable because it took place on the same day that torrential rain caused extensive flooding at Morpeth and elsewhere in Northumberland.

My wife Val and daughters Ailsa and Harriet have tolerated my preoccupation with Collingwood's officers, periodic absences from home and numerous bouts of thoughtful reflection during the past four years. They will be forgiven for breathing a collective sigh of relief that a measure of normality might now descend on the family home. Once again, regular access to the publishing and proof reading skills of my sister, Pat, has been fundamental to the success of the project. Her capacity to spot inconsistencies and errors in the text facilitated numerous amendments which undoubtedly helped to improve the final version of the book and bring it to publication. Last, but by no means least, Andrea Murphy of Business Education Publishers, has supported the project from the moment I suggested it to her and eased the burden of obtaining copyright permissions for the images held in the collections of the National Maritime Museum, Greenwich.

Collingwood's Northumbrians is dedicated to the late Tony Lea whose death in 2008, after a long illness, stoically endured, occurred as research for the book reached its end stages. Tony's sea-going career in the Merchant Navy and RFA coincided with the last 'golden age' of the British shipping industry and his memories of it cemented a friendship through countless conversations.

Tony Barrow
Embleton, Northumberland
January 2010

Biography

Tony Barrow was formerly Lecturer in History and Archaeology at Newcastle College. He is an Associate Lecturer of the Open University and a Visiting Lecturer of the University of Sunderland. He studied at Newcastle University and obtained his Ph.D from the University of Northumbria in 1989. Tony is widely consulted for his knowledge of regional ships and shipping in the age of sail, and is the author of numerous books and articles about the maritime history of the region. His other books include; *Tall Ships: Two Rivers* (with A. Osler); *Press Gangs and Privateers: Aspects of the Maritime History of North East England; Walks around the Old Coal Ports of Northumberland* and its companion volume *Walks around the Old Grain Ports of Northumberland; The Whaling Trade of North-East England 1750-1850; Britain and the Baltic: Studies in Commercial, Political and Cultural Relations 1500-2000* (Edited with P. Salmon) and *Trafalgar Geordies.*

Introduction

On the wall of the south aisle in the parish church of St. Mary the Virgin on Holy Island a simple commemoration reads: *Edward Grey, Post Captain in the Royal Navy, died November 1, 1825 aged 70*. Grey served as a midshipman in *Victory* [100] and various other warships during the American War of Independence. Years later, in March 1795, as first lieutenant of *Romulus* [36] he took part in the capture of *Ca Ira* [80] after her engagement with Nelson's *Agamemnon* [64] and was commended for his bravery.[1] In the graveyard of the same church, hidden amongst weathered headstones now impossible to read, there is a memorial to several members of the Lilburn family, all naval officers, who died on active service during the French Wars between 1793 and 1815. They represent many Northumbrian naval officers of that generation drawn from the ranks of prominent, closely connected landed families in the county. The best known, of course, is Vice-Admiral Lord Collingwood whose naval career spanned those critical years in the development of the British Empire between 1760 and 1810.

Collingwood's life and achievements have attracted numerous biographies over the years.[2] To his contemporaries he was a rather stern and reserved character, politically conservative and something of a traditionalist in his attitudes to society and its institutions. His sea-going career spanned a period of great change in the Royal Navy, particularly in the relationship between officers and men. When he entered the service in 1761 it was still common for naval commanders to have 'followers', often recruited from the captain's home district, who moved with him from ship to ship.

It was an effective means of overcoming the chronic wartime manning problem, and gave a measure of cohesion and continuity to a ship's company. By the 1790s, however, when Collingwood himself was a captain, the practice was unusual and few naval commanders were allowed such an indulgence. The greater size of the Navy and its warships, together with their ability to remain at sea for longer periods of time, created a more bureaucratic and class-ridden system in which the authority of naval officers was often enforced by harsh discipline rather than regional loyalty and mutual respect. Collingwood, a strict disciplinarian himself, condemned this trend and sought to preserve some of the conventions of the 'old' Navy. He demanded obedience but respected the men he commanded and censured officers who verbally abused seamen or regularly indulged in what he considered to be harsh or unnecessary punishment. The eminent naval historian, N.A.M. Rodger, represents Collingwood as one of a new breed of naval officer, concerned for the health and well-being of his men, who condemned excessive flogging as '…big with the most dangerous consequences and subversive to all real discipline'.[3]

At the same time, Collingwood's well known preference for officers and seamen from Northumberland reflected an earlier and more traditional practice. In September 1803, flying his flag in *Venerable*[74], Collingwood received over 200 volunteers from Tyneside on the back of his reputation as a popular and humane commander although few of them remained with him for long. Admiral Collingwood and his principal officers regularly moved from one ship to another between 1803 and 1805 so that many of these 'Newcastle volunteers' subsequently fought on other warships under different captains.

Collingwood had a particular talent for training young officers and his reputation for cultivating their careers made him a popular choice for the sons of respectable families. He encouraged them to develop a sound knowledge of navigation and practical seamanship, censured improper or immoderate language and sought to embed within their behaviour a sense of duty and responsibility befitting officers and gentlemen. If they proved to be diligent and resourceful he sought to promote them. Where they displayed indolence and a lack of motivation he advised other careers, often with a dryness of wit that characterised much of his correspondence:

> Mrs. Currel's son can never be a sailor. He has something very odd in his manner, or rather he has no manner at all…it is a pity she did not put him apprentice to Jno. Wilson the apothecary, he might have gone on very wisely…and if he did poison an old woman now and then, better do that than drown an entire ship's company…[4]

Collingwood regularly expressed critical opinions of commissioned officers as well if they did not live up to the standards of seamanship and behaviour he expected of them. Individual officers might easily damage their promotion prospects by alienating senior officers like Collingwood, either by their temperament or incompetence, displaying cowardice or indecision under fire or interrupting the continuity of their naval service. *Collingwood's Northumbrians* is an attempt to provide a context in which to understand these influences by offering a series of biographical sketches of some of the officers who served with him during their naval careers. All of them were named in his correspondence at one time or another. Chapter 1 describes the economic, social and political character of Northumberland during the eighteenth century. It explains the context of Collingwood's naval career and the central role of patronage within it. Chapter 2, Collingwood's Admiral, offers an account of the life of Admiral

Robert Roddam (1719-1808), a significant figure in Collingwood's personal and professional life. Roddam's influence extended to the highest ranks of the Admiralty and he regularly exercised it to gain promotion for Northumbrian naval officers. The character and abilities of Collingwood's flag-captain at Trafalgar, Edward Rotheram (1753-1830), the subject of Chapter 3, attracted so much criticism from the Admiral's pen that his reputation has suffered from it ever since. Rotheram was a colourful character but his temperament clearly exasperated many of the officers who served with him. Chapter 4, Collingwood's Lieutenant, is an account of the social origins and naval experience of William Landless (1762-1826) whose long and varied career eventually facilitated the purchase of property, a prosperous farm and the acquisition of gentrified status in provincial society. Collingwood's Midshipmen, Granville Thompson (1788-1817) and George Castle (1790-1826), the subjects of Chapter 5, joined the Admiral on *Venerable* in 1803 and followed him from ship to ship until after Trafalgar. Both of them subsequently became lieutenants and accumulated considerable experience of boat attacks and amphibious operations during the Peninsular War. Admiral Collingwood was a formative influence on their naval careers.

Long before the end of the Napoleonic War the Admiralty had substantially more commissioned officers than there were posts for them to fill. Those able to solicit the support of powerful patrons were usually more successful in securing commissions than those without influence or whose naval connections were undermined by the death of a senior officer. Admiral Roddam died in 1808, Edward Rotheram and William Landless retired from active service later the same year. Granville Thompson and George Castle remained lieutenants for the rest of their lives. The extent to which their careers were typical of other naval officers of that generation remains an open question. As N.A.M. Rodger has observed so perspicaciously elsewhere:

We cannot exactly tell if, or how, particular naval officers were lucky or unlucky in their careers, because we cannot say what were the normal expectations of officers of their generation.[5]

With this in mind there is an obvious utility in reconstructing the careers of *Collingwood's Northumbrians* as a way of throwing more light on the issues he raises. It also offers an opportunity to assess the roles played by the many influences affecting the promotion prospects of eighteenth century naval officers. Those that might be called 'macro' influences such as background, social class and the role of patronage and those 'micro' factors associated with the temperament, experience and abilities of individual officers. Nor should we ignore the role of contingency or that elusive quality so famously identified by Napoleon, luck.

References

1. Tracey, N., *Who's Who in Nelson's Navy*, Chatham Publishing (2006), pp. 163-165.

2. Two recent examples are Adams, M., *Nelson's own Hero: Admiral Collingwood*, Weidenfeld & Nicholson (2005) and Orde, D., *In the Shadow of Nelson: The Life of Admiral Lord Collingwood*, Pen & Sword (2008).

3. Rodger, N.A.M., *Shipboard Life in the Georgian Navy 1750-1800: The Decline of the Old Order*, Fischer, L.R., Hamre, H. and others (eds.), *The North Sea: Twelve Essays on Social History of Maritime Labour*, Stavanger Maritime Museum/Association of North Sea Societies, Stavanger (1992), p. 35.

4. Hughes, E., *The Private Correspondence of Admiral Lord Collingwood*, Navy Records Society (NRS), (1957), Admiral Collingwood to Mrs. Stead, April 1809.

5. Rodger, N.A.M., Commissioned officers' careers in the Royal Navy, 1690-1815, *Journal of Maritime History* (June 2001), p. 1.

'I have taken the liberty to send you on board a Berwick smack to be forwarded by the Portsmouth wagon a box containing half a score of fish which I beg you will do me the honour to accept and I shall be happy to execute any of your commands you may have in the North.'

[Lt. George Younghusband to Admiral Robert Roddam
19 October 1789]

Patronage, Promotion and Provincial Society in Northumberland

Northumberland at the close of the eighteenth century was a county of contrasts, reflecting in microcosm, to some degree, the economic and social character of the country as a whole. Agriculture and occupations connected with it dominated employment and the majority of people lived in small rural communities and market towns. On its southern fringe along the banks of the Tyne and the littoral districts between Blyth and Shields, the coal trade and the industrial development generated by it, such as shipbuilding, metalworking and rope-making, assumed a greater importance as the century wore on. Newcastle's role as the regional capital remained unchallenged despite the declining influence of its guilds and the growth of settlement on both banks of the Tyne. By exploiting the rights and privileges derived from its ancient charters and its control of the conservancy of the river, Newcastle dominated the coal trade and its merchants accumulated enormous wealth and political influence through their connection with it. The rise of families such as Ridley, Carr, Blackett and Ellison are perhaps the best known. Over the course of the long eighteenth century they acquired by purchase, marriage or inheritance, landed estates throughout the region and some even aspired to a peerage. Of course, fortunes might still be won or lost on the basis of politics or religion, particularly in an age of Jacobitism; this was the fate of the Radcliffes, Forsters and Fenwicks. Nevertheless, there were many other families who translated commercial wealth into land ownership while still retaining their foothold in trade. As Purdue has observed in his study of the Carr-Ellison family:

> Wealthy families were reluctant to leave behind the source of their wealth and occupied for several generations an intermediate position of merchant gentry or gentrified merchants before becoming purely landed.[1]

A landed estate, even of modest acreage, was a safe investment and conferred on its owner and his family both independence and a sense of permanence. By contrast, commercial or industrial wealth was considered less secure and prone to the vagaries of the market. Combining them offered the best of both worlds and became the preferred option for many of the landed families in the county. For example, between 1761 and 1764 Sir John Hussey Delaval, together with his brother Thomas, invested over £10,000 on harbour improvement, glassworks and coal mining at Seaton Sluice, a considerable sum by the standards of the time. Nevertheless, it trebled the capacity of the port to handle coal shipments, generated additional employment, population growth and commercial wealth. By 1770 the Seaton Delaval collieries employed over 300 pitmen and annual coal exports reached 80,000 tons in 1777.[2] During the same period Sir John improved agricultural practices on the family estate at Ford and, as the MP for Berwick for over 20 years, periodically, between 1754 and 1786, he exercised considerable political as well as economic influence in the county.

Similarly, the Ridley baronets of Blagdon Hall were, by the early years of the nineteenth century, well advanced in their transition from urban dignitaries to landed aristocracy. Much of their wealth derived from the shrewd investments of Alderman Matthew White. In 1722 he purchased from his son-in-law, Richard Ridley, the estates of Lord Widdrington and the Earl of Derwentwater in the vicinity of Blyth sequestered by the Crown following their support for the Jacobites in 1715. Once acquired, the White Ridley family sponsored industrial enterprise and harbour improvements at Blyth, invested in the first Newcastle bank, improved their estate at Blagdon and became active in local politics. Successive generations of the family sat as MPs for Newcastle and exercised an extensive patronage throughout the county.

Outside the boundaries of south-east Northumberland and the lower Tyne, however, continuity rather than change was the dominant characteristic. At the close of the eighteenth century the economy of Northumberland enjoyed a period of great prosperity. Enduring peace and political stability in the Borders was particularly significant for the expansion of cereal cultivation in Glendale, Upper Tweeddale and the farms of the coastal plain. These districts became acknowledged centres of innovation and agricultural improvement although backward farming methods and poor soils continued to be widespread until well after 1850. Contemporary commentators drew attention to the distinctive pattern of landowning in Northumberland which was, according to one local historian '… to an unusual degree a county of large estates and large farms'.[3]

The extent to which this provides an explanation for agricultural innovation in the county remains an open question but the greater profitability of improved farms justified higher rents. Landowners were also prominent in sponsoring rural industry and the construction of turnpike roads, many of them focused on the ports and market towns of the county. At Belford, Abraham Dixon IV (1723-1782), a contemporary of Sir Matthew White Ridley, inherited the surrounding estate from his father in 1746 and set about improving the local economy and infrastructure. When Arthur Young, journalist and agricultural propagandist, visited Belford in 1769 he listed a woollen mill with 16 looms, a tannery, coal mines, turnpike roads, a coaching inn (The Blue Bell) and extensive improvements to the land and its farms, concluding that:

> The spirited conduct of the present owner…the sensible attention he has given to agriculture…[and]…his judicious conduct in all matters of rural economics has brought it to the condition so flourishing to what it formerly was.[4]

Young also alluded to Dixon's attempts to develop a small port at Waren in Budle Bay for the export of local agricultural produce. At least one granary had been constructed there by 1770 and six years later Hutchinson's *History of Northumberland* was able to describe Belford as '…a small market town where great quantities of grain are sold for the export trade.'[5]

The rise of the grain trade and the export of a wide variety of agricultural produce sustained the economy of Northumberland's northern ports throughout this period. As early as 1731-32 over 51,000 quarters of grain, principally oats but increasing quantities of wheat as well, were exported from Berwick and Alnmouth and both ports grew rapidly after 1750. By the beginning of the nineteenth century Berwick ranked amongst the top ten grain exporting ports in the kingdom. By then it had become the focus of a sophisticated network of turnpike roads, carrier services and coastal shipping connecting it with local, regional and national markets. When Fuller's *History of Berwick-upon-Tweed* was published in 1799 two shipping companies, the Old Company and the Union Company, were operating 21 smacks between Berwick, London and Leith, carrying goods as well as passengers drawn from an extensive hinterland throughout Northumberland and the Scottish Borders.[6]

Market towns like Morpeth, Wooler and Alnwick prospered as they became the focus of transport links, commercial exchange, retail and professional services. Socially, they facilitated the emergence of what contemporaries called the 'middling sort' representing a wide range of incomes and occupations; tenant farmers, professionals, shopkeepers and tradesmen. The gentry mixed freely with them in the market place or at the theatre but at another level were careful to preserve their distinctiveness. Land ownership and the property associated with it was fundamental to their social status and was invariably reflected in the positions they held in both the administrative and political representation of the county.

Before the local government reforms of the Victorian era the management of county affairs was the responsibility of the Lords Lieutenant and Justices of the Peace whose official powers incorporated a variety of military, judicial and administrative duties. In both cases, the occupation of these posts was a confirmation of their existing social position and enabled them to exercise considerable powers of local patronage.[7] An appreciation of this patronage and the ways in which it was exercised is therefore fundamental to an understanding of the context of Collingwood's naval career as well as those of his officers because:

Patronage was a fact of life, as unremarkable as it was obvious, and for which a definition was neither wanted nor needed. Anyone who was ignorant of the existence, nature and importance of patronage would have been thought a fool and regarded as an object of pity.[8]

However, although wealth and the connections it brought certainly gave access to, as well as an ability to exercise, patronage, it did not always guarantee direct social or political influence, especially for the younger sons of landed families. With a good education they might construct a successful career in politics, the law or the church. Careers in medicine or trade were also considered suitable. Many younger sons of the gentry developed successful careers in the armed forces although it called for capital to purchase a commission and a substantial independent income to sustain the lifestyle associated with officers of fashionable regiments. Another popular alternative for sons of the Northumbrian gentry was to embark upon a career as an officer in the Royal Navy.

It was undoubtedly true, as the distinguished naval historian N.A.M. Rodger has observed, that 'The Navy was the only profession for a gentleman which did not require the application of money or influence.'[9] Nevertheless, access to both usually proved to be a great advantage. 'Interest', to quote another naval historian '...was deeply woven into the very fabric of the Navy.'[10]

By contrast with the problems associated with finding crews for its warships, the Admiralty never found itself short of officer recruits despite the potential dangers and discomfort of a naval life. Indeed, given the discipline, diet and poor rates of pay it might, at first, seem puzzling that the sons of the gentry, business and professional classes chose to go to sea at all. A sense of adventure or the prospect of prize money motivated some as the memoirs and correspondence of former naval officers demonstrates. Others were clearly influenced by family tradition. It remained true, however, that for many naval officers in the Georgian navy promotion could be an unpredictable and haphazard affair. Those with social and political connections might be advanced rapidly, particularly if their patrons were related and themselves senior naval officers. Others spent years on active service in the same rank with little prospect of further promotion. The political and international context also proved to be a decisive influence on the prospects of individual officers. Those who joined the Navy during a period of peace or at the end of a war, like Collingwood, might wait a long time for promotion whereas officers who joined the Navy either during or just before the outbreak of a major war could experience rapid promotion. Collingwood was 27 and had served for 14 years when he was promoted lieutenant in 1775. Nelson, who was ten years younger, became a lieutenant at 18 after only six years service and a post-captain at 20. The fact that Nelson's uncle had become Comptroller of the Navy in 1775 was clearly decisive in the process.

Nevertheless, there was always a limit to the amount of patronage that individual office holders could exercise on behalf of their dependants and supporters, particularly in the context of national politics. Parliamentary elections in the eighteenth century were notoriously corrupt by modern standards and bribery was commonplace because many electors expected to be bribed. Contested elections were therefore expensive and to be avoided if some accommodation could be reached between prospective candidates and their supporters.

In Northumberland parliamentary representation was distributed between four constituencies; the county itself and the boroughs of Newcastle, Morpeth and Berwick, each returning two MPs. Leading landowning and mercantile families naturally dominated both the selection and return of local members. At Morpeth, the Earls of Carlisle influenced the nomination of every MP who sat for the borough between 1727 and 1832. In

Northumberland it was usual for the Percy family to nominate one of the two county MPs, leaving the remaining seat to be determined by other local interests.[11]

Berwick, on the other hand, was a 'government borough' and much of the patronage associated with it enabled the sitting MP to secure military, naval, ordnance and custom house appointments for his supporters.

Amongst those entitled to vote at Berwick elections during the eighteenth century were members of the Younghusband family. They might be considered typical representatives of the Northumberland gentry with estates at Elwick, near Belford, and commercial interests in the town itself. Several generations of the family were freemen of Berwick and numbered amongst them was George Younghusband, a naval lieutenant, who became a key figure in the politics of the town. After service as a midshipman on various ships commanded by Rear-Admiral Sir Francis Geary during the Seven Years War, Younghusband was promoted lieutenant in 1761 and served in that rank until the war ended in 1763. Thereafter opportunities for further promotion were inevitably restricted.[12] By 1763 Younghusband was 31 years old and at that age he was unlikely to be preferred to officers younger than himself without the support of an influential patron. Accordingly, in 1764, he became an active supporter of Sir John Hussey Delaval who represented Berwick in parliament.

Lieutenant Younghusband acted as Sir John's electoral agent at Berwick for almost 30 years and the surviving correspondence between them clearly demonstrates both the expectations of an active political supporter as well as the constraints imposed on a sitting MP in his attempts to satisfy them. Some burgesses expected, and usually received, monetary reward before they pledged their votes, as well as appointments to government posts once a parliamentary candidate had been elected.[13] In George Younghusband's case he consistently solicited Delaval to use his influence to have him promoted and commissioned to command a naval vessel in home waters. During Sir John's second term as MP for Berwick, from 1764-74, he was able to satisfy these expectations when Younghusband was appointed to *Adventure* [12]. In a letter of September 1767 Younghusband acknowledged his debt of gratitude:

> As your absence from Ford prevents me from returning my thanks in person for the trouble you have given yourself in procuring me the command of the *Adventure* cutter, (which I received my commission for on Monday), I take this method in doing it and answering you that I shall make use of every opportunity in my power of expressing my gratitude.[14]

The following month, after the Admiralty had ordered him to exchange stations with a similar vessel based on a different part of the coast, he wrote again to Sir John requesting him to '…make application to get me re-instated to my former station or appointed to the *Alarm* to which I have no objection on the old station (Orkneys to Isle of Skye)'. Once again, Delaval's representations proved to be successful and Younghusband remained in command of *Alarm* [4] until the outbreak of the American War of Independence.[15] By this time, however, Sir John was out of favour with the government and had been defeated at the General Election in 1774. It considerably reduced his powers of patronage and his ability to reward Younghusband's continuing support. In 1775 he was superseded in command of *Alarm* and subsequently spent most of the American War as a lieutenant of press gangs at Berwick and Leith. Both were positions of lower status and few prospects '…the most disagreeable service a lieutenant can be employed in'. Despite numerous letters to Sir John requesting him to use his interest with the Admiralty to have him promoted he remained at Edinburgh until the end of the war:

In November 1776, I was appointed upon the Impress Service at Berwick but in consequence of my attachment to your interest I was ordered to brick-up my Rendezvous and dismiss my gang when I had only been employed seventeen days and through Lord Lisburn, Lieutenant Joseph Stevenson was afterwards appointed... . As I persuaded myself that I spared neither trouble nor expense in supporting your interest these years past I fear that my family will fail. I could not have believed but you would make a point of providing for me with the first of your friends... [and] ...flattered myself you would have got me promoted as I may without vanity say my services deserved it and have only now to request that you will candidly inform me if you have any prospect of getting me promoted soon.[16]

Sir John Delaval was elected as MP for Berwick for a third time in 1780 and was perceived by the government to be an important influence amongst the independents of the country gentry. He appears to have been promised an Irish peerage in return for his support and clearly enjoyed the prospect of extending renewed patronage to his supporters. However, despite his positive relationship with Lord North's government, Delaval continued to experience obstacles in his efforts to reward Younghusband's loyalty. In 1785-86 he unsuccessfully lobbied Pitt for command of a Falmouth packet and discovered that his representations to the Admiralty had been ignored because of Lord Howe's opposition.[17]

Howe alleged that Younghusband had been responsible for financial misdemeanours and false accounting during his service at Leith. Sir John wrote:

Lord Howe objected to you for having made false account when employed on the Impress Service and although I will continue to make representations on your behalf...the last answer I received was that Lord Howe would not appoint any lieutenant to a cutter who had made up an account in the manner that you did.[18]

Younghusband's vehement denial of the accusation was eventually accepted at the Admiralty and in 1789 he was given command of *Kite* [12], a Customs cutter on the North Sea station, patrolling between Flamborough and St. Abbs Head. 'The cutter does not sail very fast', he wrote to Sir John, 'but I hope to have the good fortune to take a few prizes in her.'[19] It is not known whether he was successful in doing so. By 1790 he was clearly more concerned to use what influence he had on behalf of his four sons, all of whom pursued careers in the armed forces, three of them in the Royal Navy. Sir John Delaval remained his principal patron but his letter to Admiral Roddam from Berwick in 1789, with a gift of Tweed salmon, indicated a long established interest in cultivating the patronage of the Admiral as well. His sons' entry into the Royal Navy undoubtedly benefited from the connections he cultivated through Admiral Roddam, a popular and highly respected naval officer, who exercised considerable influence at the Admiralty. Younghusband knew this very well and his present of a box of fish was a symbol of it.[20]

Robert Roddam (1719-1808) was a key figure in advancing the careers of a number of Northumbrian naval officers although that of Cuthbert Collingwood was undoubtedly the most successful and best known. Roddam enjoyed a long and distinguished naval career lasting almost 60 years and, as Admiral of the Red, came to exert what the distinguished naval historian, Michael Lewis, deemed to be:

'One of the most powerful forms of service interest that could be exercised on behalf of a junior officer', adding that, 'it is not easy to see this form of interest in action because, from the nature of it, it was somewhat back stair, [nevertheless] the young officer who had the interest of one of these "great ones" behind him was very fortunate indeed'.[21]

Roddam's patronage was extensive as well as effective and a number of Northumberland naval families, particularly in the north of the county, benefited from it. These included the Lilburn and Selby families of Holy Island as well as the Younghusband family at Berwick. At least three generations of Lilburns served in the Royal Navy in the century between 1760 and 1860 and Roddam's early influence on their fortunes was acknowledged by the family who gave the name, Robert Roddam Lilburn, to younger sons over two generations.[22]

Admiral Roddam's patronage of Cuthbert Collingwood began when he was captain of *Lenox* [74] at Portsmouth in 1772 although they were distantly related and shared a previous naval connection. Both were members of old Northumberland families and their friendship was consolidated by Collingwood's marriage to Sarah Blackett in 1791.[23] However, since there was no tradition of naval service on the Collingwood side of the family when he entered the Navy in 1761, he did so under the protection of his cousin, Captain (later Admiral) Richard Brathwaite. He was a near contemporary of Admiral Roddam and, like Roddam, had also served under Admiral Chaloner Ogle in the West Indies during the 1740s. Collingwood, who served under Brathwaite in various ships for almost ten years, acknowledged the debt he owed to him in a memoir of January 1806:

[His] regard for me, and the interest which he took in whatever related to my improvement in nautical knowledge, I owe great obligation.[24]

Admiral Robert Roddam (1719-1808)
[Lemuel Abbot]
Painted about 1783 when Roddam was the port-admiral at Chatham. He wears a
flag officer's full dress uniform of that period and a wig. Roddam had a long and
distinguished naval career and used his considerable influence at the Admiralty
to promote the careers of numerous Northumbrian naval officers including
Collingwood and Landless.
[National Maritime Museum]

Roddam Hall
Admiral Roddam inherited the family estates on the death of his brother, Edward, in 1776. He took a particular interest in Roddam Hall and its surroundings which included gardens, woodland walks and a boating lake.
[Author's Collection with permission of Lord & Lady Vinson]

Roddam Family Mausoleum at Ilderton
Admiral Roddam was the last representative of a Northumberland family that had farmed in the foothills of The Cheviot since Saxon times. At his death in 1808 the estate passed to a distant relative on condition that he took the name Roddam.
[Author's Collection]

Warships off Portsmouth Harbour
[J.W. Carmichael]

A lively scene depicting several types of warship common in the sailing navy. On the left a frigate shortens sail as she prepares to enter the harbour while, in the centre, a ship of the line heels before a favourable breeze and heads for the open sea. The vessel on the right is a naval cutter of the type that Lieutenant George Younghusband commanded in the North Sea between 1767 and 1774.

[Courtesy of Tyne Wear Archives and Museums]

Dreadnought 104 guns, at present lying off Greenwich for the Seamen's Hospital
[A.W. Cooke]
A fine sketch of Collingwood's former flagship and Trafalgar veteran which reveals the massive bulk of a ship of the line of Nelson's navy. Collingwood's Northumbrians all served together in *Dreadnought* in 1804-05. She was used as a floating hospital off Greenwich between 1827 and 1856.
[National Maritime Museum]

Collingwood's Captain: Edward Rotheram (1753-1830)
Collingwood frequently expressed his contempt for Rotheram's temperament and abilities but never questioned his courage and experience of battle. Rotheram was commissioned as captain of *Bellerophon* after Trafalgar and remained in command of her until 1808. Thereafter he had no further service at sea.

The day after Trafalgar. Royal Sovereign under tow of Euryalus
[Nicholas Pocock]
One of a series of water colours depicting the aftermath of the battle. *Royal Sovereign* subsequently lost her one remaining mast during the gale of 24/25 October 1805 and Rotheram later recalled that his ship "came very near foundering in the gale from shot holes and loss of masts".
[National Maritime Museum]

Rotheram's grave at Bildeston in Suffolk
After his death in 1830 Rotheram was buried in an unmarked grave until 1890-91 when a subscription was raised to have a memorial stone placed over it. There is also a commemorative plaque inside the church.
[Author's Collection]

The Battle of the Saintes, 12 April 1782

[Thomas Luny]

The painting depicts an incident at the close of the battle as *Ville de Paris*, de Grasse's flagship (centre), is engaged with Admiral Rodney's *Formidable* (right). De Grasse finally surrendered to Admiral Hood's *Barfleur* which can be seen across the bows of both ships. Rotheram in *Monarch* and Landless in *Royal Oak* were both present at the battle.

[National Maritime Museum]

Extract from the journal of the *Monarch*, at Battle of the Saintes 12 April 1782

Monarch suffered amongst the highest casualties sustained by a British ship at the Battle of the Saintes, 16 killed and 33 wounded. Rotheram was unscathed and his promotion to lieutenant was confirmed when his ship returned to England.
(The National Archives)

Admiral Lord Collingwood
[J. Lonsdale]
"Collingwood, in short, take him all in all, will perhaps stand second to none
that ever hoisted a flag". (Landsman Hay) Collingwood had a particular talent
for training young naval officers but was critical of those who failed to meet his
exacting standards of discipline and behaviour.
[Courtesy of Tyne Wear Archives and Museums]

Collingwood served under Roddam for only a year but thereafter the Admiral exercised a direct influence on his career, first recommending him to Admiral Sir Samuel Graves under whom he served in North America and subsequently to Admiral Sir Peter Parker, when he commanded a fleet in the West Indies. It was Admiral Parker who promoted Collingwood commander of *Badger* [14] in 1778 and then post-captain of the frigate *Hinchinbroke* [28] in 1779. Fifteen years later, in 1794, a brief exchange of correspondence between Roddam and Admiral George Bowyer revealed Roddam's continuing influence in promoting Collingwood's career following his service as flag-captain to Bowyer in *Barfleur* [98] at the Battle of the Glorious First of June.[25]

In 1805, after Trafalgar, Roddam expressed his satisfaction that Collingwood had:

> Finally proved himself deserving of the high opinion I early formed of him and which I always hoped would in time render him as much approved by his countrymen as he is valued by me.[26]

As Collingwood's naval career prospered he came to exercise his own service interest on behalf of the officers recommended to him and his correspondence is full of examples of his opinions of some of the young gentlemen sent to him by friends or relations, including Admiral Roddam. It is clear, however, that his desire to satisfy a patron like Roddam sometimes took precedence over his personal opinion of the character and competence of the individual officers involved. Two contrasting examples from the same year seem to illustrate this point very well.

In 1806 Collingwood promoted a certain Charles Haultain, then an 18-year-old midshipman, to lieutenant, but much against his better judgement.

'My conscience reproved me when I promoted him', he wrote, 'which I made two or three attempts to do before I could bring myself to it. Nothing but it being Admiral Roddam's request could have induced me.' Haultain was a relation of Collingwood's wife but '…the dullest lad as I ever saw and now Captain Lechmere tells me that he is so entirely useless that he is afraid he must try him by a court martial to get rid of him'.[27]

Collingwood rarely minced his words in his assessment of those he deemed to be bad officers and Haultain was no exception:

> It is this kind of person that causes all the accidents, the loss of ships, the dreadful expense of them, mutinies, insubordination and everything bad. They must produce a certificate that they are twenty one years of age, which they generally write themselves so they begin with forgery, proceed with knavery and end with perjury.[28]

Six months later Collingwood wrote:

> Pray tell Admiral Roddam that I am afraid I shall not be able to save Haultain from destruction: he has twice been in confinement and I have been obliged to write and soothe his captain to save him from a court martial. I would remove him to another ship but nobody will take him and his messmates do not associate with him.[29]

Collingwood's sense of obligation to Admiral Roddam clearly overrode his reluctance to promote a person he considered to be a bad officer and demonstrates the power of patronage as it was exercised in the Georgian navy. By contrast, earlier the same year, in March 1806, Collingwood wrote an agitated letter to Lord Barham, then First Lord of the Admiralty, expressing his disappointment that another one of his officers, Lieutenant William Landless, 'the only officer whom I recommended to your Lordships', had been overlooked in the round of promotions that followed Trafalgar. Collingwood wrote several further letters in favour of Landless and clearly felt aggrieved that the Admiralty had ignored his repeated requests to promote '…this old and valuable officer [and] thereby denying to my dependants what was so liberally given to other officers in the fleet'.[30]

Landless was undoubtedly a competent and experienced officer and his Northumbrian background was an added advantage to an admiral well known for his preference towards officers from his native Northumberland. But Landless was third lieutenant of *Dreadnought* [98] and had only served under Collingwood for just over two years, from August 1803 until October 1805. Nevertheless, Collingwood's anxiety to have him promoted clearly derived from the same obligation he felt towards Admiral Roddam as he did in the case of Haultain.

The problem for the Admiralty was that long before the end of the Napoleonic War there were substantially more commissioned officers than there were posts for them to fill. Senior naval officers like Nelson, Collingwood and St. Vincent all believed that whenever commissions became available they should be awarded to deserving officers who had distinguished themselves in the service. At the same time they recognised the greater importance of political and parliamentary influence in the preferment of naval officers as the Napoleonic War progressed. When Earl St. Vincent retired from active service in March 1807 he told King George III that:

> A sprinkling of nobility was very desirable in the Navy, as it gives some sort of consequence to the service; but at present the Navy is so overrun by the younger branches of nobility, and the sons of Members of Parliament, and they so swallow up all the patronage, and so choke up the channel to promotion, that the son of an old officer, however meritorious their services may have been, has little or no chance of getting on.[31]

In the years following Trafalgar Collingwood, as Commander-in-Chief Mediterranean Fleet, became responsible for the fortunes of thousands of officers and men and he was regularly solicited with requests to promote some of them. At the same time he recognised, but lamented, the trend towards political preferment and the pressures it created in the naval hierarchy. He wrote to his wife in December 1806:

> The vacancies which happen are in no proportion to the applicants for them. I have not made a captain, except Landless, since this time twelve months, nor has a lieutenant been removed from my ship, except one, who, seeing very little prospect of succeeding here, applied to go home and seek his fortune elsewhere.[32]

Where he could, he rewarded those he considered worthy of his confidence. Richard Thomas, who served as his signal lieutenant in *Excellent* [74], became his flag-captain. George Foggo, a former midshipman from Newcastle, who had served with Collingwood in *Barfleur* at the Glorious First of June, became his gunner on *Ocean* [110] in 1808. He promoted another young, Newcastle born midshipman, Granville Thompson, in October 1809, for conspicuous gallantry during an action with two French gun-brigs off Marseilles. A week after he promoted Thompson, Collingwood summed up his thoughts in a letter to his former first lieutenant, James Clavell:

> The truth is he [Lord Mulgrave, First Lord of the Admiralty] is so pressed by persons having parliamentary influence, that he cannot find himself at liberty to select those whose nautical skill and gallantry would otherwise present them as proper men for the service. A hole or two in the skin will not weigh against a vote in parliament.[33]

Few of the thousands of officers who served in the Georgian navy during the French Wars rose to the highest command as Collingwood did. In this sense he was not typical of the officers who served with him although much of his career conformed to recognised norms. For the majority of naval officers their entry to the Navy and subsequent promotion within it was always heavily dependent on political and professional patronage although the balance between them leaned increasingly towards the former as the nineteenth century wore on.

References

1. Purdue, A.W., *The Carrs and the Ellisons*, Sunderland University Press, (1999), p. xviii.

2. Linsley, S., *Ports and Harbours of Northumberland*, Tempus Publishing, (2005), p. 183.

3. McCord, N., *North East England: The Region's Development 1760-1960*, Batsford, (1979), p. 28.

4. Young, A., *A Six Months Tour through the North of England*, [n.pub.], (1771).

5. Hutchinson, W., *A View of Northumberland*, 2 Vols., (1776), Vol. I. p. 455.

6. Barrow, T., Corn, Carriers and Coastal Shipping: The Shipping and Trade of Berwick and the Borders, 1730-1830, *Journal of Transport History*, Vol. 21, 1, (March 2000), pp. 6-27.

7. McCord, N. & Purdue, B., *British History 1815-1914*, Oxford University Press (2007), pp. 75-76.

8. Bourne, J.M., Patronage and Society in 19th Century England cited in Greenhill & Giffard, *Steam, Politics and Patronage: The Transformation of the Royal Navy 1815-54*, Conway Maritime Press, (1994), p. 76.

9. Rodger, N.A.M., *The Wooden World: An Anatomy of the Georgian Navy*, Collins, (1986), p. 254.

10. Lewis, M., *A Social History of the Navy*, Allen and Unwin, (1960), p. 223.

11.   Speck, W.A., Northumberland Elections in the Eighteenth Century, *Northern History*, XXVIII, (1992), pp. 164-177.

12.   Rodger, N.A.M., Commissioned officers' careers in the Royal Navy, 1690-1815, *Journal of Maritime History*, (June 2001), pp. 122.

13.   Brenchley, D., Beith, A. and others, *Berwick in Parliament*, Berwick-upon-Tweed History Society (BHS), (2001), p. 21.

14.   Northumberland Record Office (NRO), 2DE 45/1/3. Lt. George Younghusband to Sir John Delaval, 22 September 1767.

15.   NRO, 2DE 45/1/1. Lt. George Younghusband to Sir John Delaval, 23 October 1767.

16.   NRO, 2DE 45/1/30. Lt. George Younghusband to Sir John Delaval, 31 March 1782. See also Brenchley, D., Beith, A. and others, *Berwick in Parliament*, BHS, (2001) pp. 78-79.

17.   Falmouth packets were small, fast, lightly armed vessels employed by the Post Office to carry bullion, passengers and confidential correspondence. Appointments to command a post office packet were highly prized and much sought after.

18.   NRO, 2DE 45/14/85. Sir John Delaval to Lt. George Younghusband, 1 June 1786.

19.   NRO, 2DE 45/14/112. Lt. George Younghusband to Sir John Delaval, 8 June 1789.

20.   George Younghusband died at Elwick in 1792 but his wife continued to write to Lord Delaval in support of the promotion of her sons, the eldest of whom, George Younghusband, became a lieutenant with Delaval's assistance in 1794 at the age of 18, and eventually a post-captain. The youngest son, appropriately called Delaval Younghusband, died at sea in 1826.

21.   Lewis, *Social History*, p. 205.

22.   Three sons of Robert Lilburn R.N. (1751-1819) followed their father into the service but none of them survived the French Wars. James Lilburn (1776-1812), first lieutenant of *Swiftsure* [74] at Trafalgar, was promoted commander in 1806 but killed at Malaga whilst captain of *Goshawk* [16]. His elder brother, Richard Lilburn (1773-1796) was also a commander but died at sea when captain of *L'Expedition* [12]. The youngest, Robert Roddam Lilburn (1787-1806) was midshipman of *L'Heureux* [22] and drowned when she foundered in the Atlantic.

23. Sarah's mother was a Roddam of Hethpool and niece of Alexander Collingwood, d. 1758.

24. Orde, D., *In the Shadow of Nelson: the Life of Admiral Lord Collingwood*, Pen & Sword (2008), p. 55.

25. NRO, ZBL 228, Admiral George Bowyer to Admiral Robert Roddam, 11 October 1794.

26. Murray, G., *Life of Admiral Collingwood*, Hutchinson, (1936), p. 28.

27. Lewis, *Social History*, p. 224.

28. Hughes, E., *The Private Correspondence of Admiral Lord Collingwood*, Navy Records Society (NRS) (1957), Collingwood to his sister, May 1806.

29. Lewis, *Social History*, p. 224.

30. Newnham Collingwood, G.L., *A Selection from the Public and Private Correspondence of Vice-Admiral Lord Collingwood, interspersed with Memoirs of his Life*, (1829), Admiral Collingwood to Lord Barham, 28 March 1806.

31. Rodger, Commissioned officers' careers in the Royal Navy, 1690-1815, p. 17.

32. Newnham Collingwood, *Public and Private Correspondence*, Admiral Lord Collingwood to Lady Collingwood, 20 December 1806.

33. *Public and Private Correspondence*, Admiral Collingwood to Commander James Clavell, 20 October 1809.

'I have received and read your letter of 28th past giving an account of your arrival at Plymouth with H.M. sloop under your command and a French privateer of six carriage guns and eight swivel guns which you took off The Start and am to acquaint you that their Lordships are pleased with your dilgence.'

[Secretary to the Admiralty to Commander Robert Roddam
1 January 1747]

Collingwood's Admiral

Robert Roddam 1719-1808

Roddam was an old Northumbrian surname with a pre-conquest ancestry dating from the reign of King Athelstan who granted Pole Roddam land at Roddam near Wooler in the tenth century. The Lay Subsidy Roll of 1296 listed numerous descendants with land throughout north Northumberland but the focus of the Roddam estates was always the foothills of the Cheviots between the Glen and the Breamish where they held a common boundary with those of Lilburn, Collingwood and Grey, all names of significance in the history of Northumberland. It was a turbulent frontier zone during the Middle Ages and suffered from the depredations of border rievers throughout the early modern period. Before the eighteenth century it was marginal land where farming was both difficult and dangerous '…because of the spoyles and wasts [sic] made by the incursions of the Scots and much barren land…which in those times might not be thought valuable'.[1]

Robert Roddam was destined to become the last male representative of the family although this seemed unlikely in his youth. As the second son of Edward Roddam his elder brother, also Edward, was bound to inherit the estate on his father's death. Accordingly, Robert pursued a career in the Navy. He entered on board *Lowestoffe* [20] in 1735 and spent five years in the West Indies. Sir Chaloner Ogle later took him into his flagship prior to the abortive expedition to capture Cartagena in March-April 1741, where, according to one antiquarian biography, Roddam narrowly escaped death and showed himself to be '…a young sailor of great valour and intrepidity'.[2]

Soon after, in November 1741, Roddam was promoted third lieutenant of *Superb* [60], Captain Hon. William Hervey. It must have been a difficult posting for a young lieutenant beginning to make a name for himself in the Navy. *Superb* was not a happy ship; the lieutenants quarrelled violently and Hervey acquired an unenviable reputation as a tempestuous and unpredictable character '…austere in his disposition, even to a degree of cruelty, [who] became at once an object both of terror and hatred to his people'.[3] Another historian has even suggested that Hervey was mentally unbalanced![4]

Whatever his true state of mind Hervey's brutal methods regularly attracted the censure of his commanding officers, 'There is no government in that ship,' Admiral Cavendish wrote in October 1740, 'the men run away with the boats and will not obey their officers. Something must be done or that ship is lost to the service'.[5]

Later, in May 1741 just before Roddam joined the ship, Admiral Vernon added his own criticism of Hervey for '…the want of good order and discipline on board the *Superb* under your command'.[6]

It was during this period that Roddam gained the acquaintance of the captain's nephew, the celebrated Augustus Hervey,[7] who was then serving as a young lieutenant in his uncle's ship. Their joint experience taught them a valuable lesson in how not to command a ship. Soon after *Superb* returned to England in 1742 Captain Hervey faced a court martial and was censured and dismissed for 'unreasonable harshness' in his treatment of officers and men. His conviction was based largely on the evidence provided by Lieutenant Roddam. A few months later, in September 1742, Roddam was commissioned to *Monmouth* [64] as third lieutenant. While cruising off Tenerife in 1744 *Monmouth* had the good fortune to capture a rich Spanish prize valued at more than £100,000. As a lieutenant, Roddam's share of the prize money amounted to several thousand pounds.

In July 1746 he was promoted commander and commissioned to *Viper* [14] a new sloop then fitting out at Poole. Roddam quickly gained the notice of no less an officer than Admiral George Anson, by then a national hero after his return from an epic circumnavigation with the silver cargo of a Spanish treasure ship. Anson had been appointed to command the Western Squadron and asked his captains at Portsmouth to recommend an officer who would sail to Plymouth in an unfavourable south-westerly gale to stop the ships based there from sailing to the French coast. Roddam volunteered and succeeded in reaching Plymouth in time to prevent them from putting to sea. Anson is said to have been so impressed with Roddam's courage and seamanship that he asked for him to be transferred to his command. Later the same year Roddam was commended for his conspicuous bravery in attacking 30 vessels laden with naval stores lying in Cedeira Bay near Cape

Ortegal. After first silencing the coastal battery protecting the anchored store ships, Roddam succeeded in sinking or damaging all of the vessels lying there and returned to the fleet with four prizes '...not being able to man more from his little sloop of fourteen guns and ninety men'.[8] He was feted as a hero and offered a seat in parliament as MP for Dartmouth but he declined the honour. Roddam attracted attention to himself again in the winter of 1746 when *Viper* engaged and captured a French privateer off Start Point whilst on convoy protection duties on the Devon coast. On this occasion the Secretary to the Admiralty was instructed 'to acquaint you that their Lordships are pleased with your diligence'.[9]

Roddam was promoted post-captain in July 1747 and commissioned to the frigate *Greyhound* [24] a ship he commanded until 1751, first in home waters and later, after 1749, on the American station. Soon after his arrival at New York Roddam outraged colonial society when he met and eloped with the daughter of the Governor, Sir Henry George Clinton. The couple were married soon after. Clinton, himself an admiral, became Governor of New York in 1743 and periodically used the military resources of the State to support the war against the French in Quebec. He sent artillery to British troops engaged in the Siege of Louisburg in 1745 and the following year successfully negotiated an anti-French alliance with the Iroquois. As a reward for their loyalty, Clinton extended colonial protection to them in 1748.

Clinton's relationship with the politicians of the New York Assembly was less cordial and he struggled to exercise his authority as Governor in the face of their concerted opposition. Clinton's nemesis was James de Lancey, Chief Justice of New York, who led a powerful group of liberal assemblymen. De Lancey was an astute politician determined to reduce the powers of the Governor and transfer them to the New York Assembly. In the context of this ongoing political war of attrition, Roddam became embroiled in a legal crisis which went to the heart of the dispute between Clinton and de Lancey.

In June 1750, while Roddam was ashore on business, the first lieutenant of *Greyhound* in an attempt to enforce a requirement that vessels dip their ensign as a courtesy to British warships, ordered the gunner's mate, James Parks, to fire a shot across the bows of a private yacht which had disregarded this convention. After the warning was ignored a second shot was fired and one of the passengers in the yacht, a maidservant called Elizabeth Sibbins, was killed. The owner of the yacht, Colonel Ricketts, a man of some substance in New York, protested to de Lancey who ordered an inquest and promptly arrested and imprisoned the seaman involved.

The affair placed Roddam in a difficult situation. As the captain of one of the King's ships he petitioned de Lancey for the release of the man and cited the royal prerogatives exercised by the Governor in his defence. However, since George Clinton was by now his father-in-law, soliciting his support left Roddam vulnerable to charges that familial influence rather than legal rights lay at the root of his demand. De Lancey held firm despite several letters from Roddam:

> Your gunner's mate is charged with the murder of Elizabeth Sibbins committed within the city and county of New York, therefore cannot comply with your demand to deliver up to you your gunner's mate.

With a hint of sarcasm rather than sympathy, de Lancey turned the knife a little more:

> I am sorry this accident has given you so much trouble. It is likely to give some more as it is a case of great consequence and requires great consideration.[10]

Roddam wrote to the Admiralty describing his predicament and seeking their advice but he was unlikely to receive a reply before October. In the meantime he refused to surrender Lieutenant How, the officer who gave the order to fire, and had him transferred to *Hector* [44] then under orders to sail for England. De Lancey protested:

> I would recommend to you to consider the consequences of this proceeding and how far by it you make yourself accessory to the crime charged upon him.[11]

Whether Roddam heeded this advice and hesitated to send his first lieutenant back to England is unclear although he appears to have anticipated the Admiralty's orders which finally arrived in December. The legal impasse between Clinton and de Lancey was eventually resolved by the adjudication of the Attorney-General who concluded:

> So far as I can judge from the account of the evidence, I apprehend that the lieutenant and the gunner's mate are guilty of murder and that the proper place for the trial is at the Admiralty Commissioners.[12]

De Lancey was deemed to have exceeded his legal authority in committing and detaining Parks; Clinton was instructed to secure his release. Both the gunner's mate and Lieutenant How were returned to England to stand trial. Roddam's stance in the dispute was vindicated but any satisfaction he may have felt must have been tempered by a sense of personal loss. Roddam's father died soon after his arrival on the American station and his wife, Lucy Clinton, who had never enjoyed good health, died just as the legal dispute was resolved.

Greyhound returned to England and paid off at Deptford in September 1751. Captain Roddam took the opportunity to return to Northumberland to visit his elder brother who had inherited the family estate during his absence in America. He returned to active service in 1753 accepting a commission to command *Bristol* [50] the guard ship at Plymouth.

In 1755 as war with France threatened yet again, Roddam was commissioned to command *Greenwich* [50] and promptly sailed for the West Indies. He read the official declaration of war against France to the ship's company at Port Royal, Jamaica, on 23 August 1756.[13] Since desertion and disease were perennial problems for the officers of British warships stationed in the West Indies the declaration of war was not universally popular amongst seamen in the fleet. In December 1756 there were several courts martial for desertion, insubordination and mutiny and a number of seamen suffered the ultimate penalty under the Articles of War. On 20 December the log of *Greenwich* recorded that:

> At half past nine hoisted a yellow flag at the foretopmasthead and fired a gun. At half past ten read the Articles of War and John Boyd was hanged at this ship's foreyardarm pursuant to his sentence. At eleven John Boyd was lowered down into the yawl and carried to be buried.[14]

Neal Smith, another seaman, received 150 lashes the following day and in January 1757 William Phillips a seaman of *Dreadnought* [60] sentenced to death for mutiny received a last minute reprieve '…the prisoner being pardoned and ordered to return to his proper place'.[15] Presumably by that time Rear-Admiral Townsend considered that he had made enough examples of recalcitrant seamen to prevent further outbreaks of mutiny and insubordination. Soon after *Greenwich* sailed from Port Royal under orders from Rear-Admiral Townsend to:

> Cruize [sic] between Cape Francois and the Old Cape on the south side of Hispaniola for two months or as long as your provisions will last…and should you gain

any intelligence of the arrival of any French Men-of - War you are immediately to joyn [sic] me at Port Royal.[16]

During the morning of 16 March while patrolling off Cape Cabron, Hispaniola, *Greenwich* was sighted by a French squadron of superior force consisting of five ships of the line, two frigates and an armed store ship. Roddam cleared for action and steered close inshore '…as I knew that if they were Men-of-War it was the only method I could take to get clear'.[17]

Greenwich was hopelessly outnumbered and in light winds there was little prospect of out-manoeuvring the French ships. By mid-afternoon *L'Eville* [64] passed within point blank range 'and fired as long as her guns would reach'. Finally:

> At eight with a sixty four close astern and a seventy four and a frigate nearby I knew they must in half an hour be all alongside me and that I should then have no chance of escaping. It was the opinion of all of my officers that I had done all that could have been done for H.M. Service and that our engaging any longer could only tend to sacrificing the people. I therefore ordered the colours to be struck.[18]

Roddam's account was corroborated by his first lieutenant, Isaac Crouch, as well as the other officers and men called in his defence. The court martial unanimously declared that the capture of *Greenwich* had been unavoidable and that Roddam had done everything in his power to preserve the ship. He was acquitted with honour.

In December 1759, after his return to England, Roddam was commissioned to command *Colchester* [50] then patrolling off Ushant as part of Admiral Lord Hawke's Western Squadron. With the French planning an invasion and 21 ships of the line at Brest preparing to put to sea, the situation was serious and everything depended upon the success of Hawke's blockade. A procession of strong gales in early June drove the British ships back to Torbay but they also prevented French warships from leaving Brest so that when the weather moderated in early July, Hawke was able to resume his station off Ushant and re-establish his blockade.

Amongst the British captains under his command was Augustus Hervey with whom Roddam had briefly served as a lieutenant in *Superb*. Hervey in *Monmouth* and Captain Lendrick in *Montague* [60] were ordered to stand in close to Brest harbour to observe the preparations of the French fleet and at the same time '…not to suffer a neutral vessel of any nation whatsoever to enter the port'.[19]

But this was easier said than done. The coast of Brittany presented challenging obstacles to the safe navigation of large sailing warships. It is strewn with submerged rocks and small islands where strong tides, unpredictable weather and inaccurate charts combined to increase the risk of damage or even shipwreck. A general increase in the size and capacity of sailing warships during the eighteenth century together with the emergence of an efficient means of victualling them, undoubtedly improved their seaworthiness and ability to remain on station in the Western Approaches, but storm damage and navigational errors continued to be constant dangers. The loss of *Magnificent* [74] and the frigate *Hussar* [38] on uncharted rocks in 1804 were prescient reminders of the treacherous nature of that coast.

Patrolling the approaches to Brest demanded courage as well as skill and Hervey possessed both in good measure. When four French ships of the line crept out of Brest harbour at dawn on 22 July 1759 hoping to take Hervey's ships by surprise they were spotted immediately and, although they were outnumbered two to one, the British ships cleared for action:

> I have but just time to tell you by the cutter that four
> sail of the enemy's ships are now out of the Road laying

to, which is to be drive us off (the others not moving) and then to get their convoy in from Conquet. The *Colchester* and a frigate is in sight, therefore we will not be drove off easily.[20]

Colchester and the frigate had been detached from Hawke's main fleet to give support. Hervey signalled to them several times to make more sail and close up to him but neither of them did so. When the cutter reached Hawke's fleet and four more ships were detached to support, the French had second thoughts and put back to Brest before Hervey was close enough to bring them to action. Why *Colchester* failed to make sail earlier than she did remains an open question and it drew some critical remarks from Hervey's biographer, Tim Clayton, who observed:

> The clear implication of Thomas' minutes [Reynold Thomas was Hervey's clerk] is that Hervey thought *Colchester*'s officers either culpably unobservant or unwilling to sacrifice themselves.[21]

It seems likely that her captain was censured and subsequently removed for his neglect and Roddam commissioned to *Colchester* in his place. In early 1760 when ordered to relieve Captain Duff patrolling off Belle Isle, Roddam carried *Colchester* through the Passage du Raz between the Saintes and the shore '…believed to be the first English ship ever to make the attempt'.[22]

Later he sailed to St. Helena to escort a convoy of East India Company ships back to England and soon after his return the Treaty of Paris ended the Seven Years War. *Colchester* was paid off and Roddam returned to his home in Northumberland.

Over the next seven years, together with his brother Edward, he devoted himself to the administration and improvement of the family estates at Roddam and Little Houghton. He took an active interest in the construction of Roddam Hall, an elegant Georgian house set in its own landscaped grounds. His improvements included plantations, woodland walks and a boating lake as well as an impressive tree-lined approach road known as Admiral's Avenue, still marked on modern Ordnance Survey maps.[23] The estate of Roddam and Threestoneburn exceeded 3,000 acres, more than half of which consisted of grouse moor and rough pasture in the foothills of Hedgehope and The Cheviot. Arable cultivation came to be focused on three estate farms called Mount Athelstan, Rigg House and Calder described in 1816 as '…containing 1,200 acres of rich turnip and barley soil in a high state of cultivation'.[24] Another farm at Branton in the Breamish valley near Ingram was leased by Roddam to Alexander and William Brown in February 1764.[25]

Roddam's farms were located in a district of north Northumberland well known for its agricultural improvers. George and Matthew Culley became close neighbours and no doubt regular visitors, when they purchased the tenancy of a farm at Fenton in 1767. Another successful agriculturalist, John Grey of Milfield, widely acknowledged for his contribution to improvements in Glendale, also lived within a few miles. Roddam, clearly motivated by a similar spirit of innovation, insisted that his tenants be restricted to seven-year leases as a way of consolidating his improvements and maximising the rental income of his farms. Roddam acquired further estates near Gillingham in Kent after his marriage to Alithea, sister of the future Admiral Sir Robert Calder, in 1769. Roddam returned to naval service during the Falkland Islands crisis of the following year and served as captain of *Lenox* the guardship at Portsmouth until 1773. In 1776 Roddam inherited the family estate in his own right on the death of his elder brother, Edward.

In March 1777 with the American War of Independence going badly and the prospect of France joining it as an ally of the rebellious colonists, Roddam accepted a commission to take command of *Cornwall* [74] at Chatham. Lord North's government faced difficult times. Bringing more ships into commission was one thing but finding seamen to man them was quite another. Press gangs were constantly on the lookout for skilled mariners on shore as well as at sea where most pressing was usually done. Frigates and naval cutters regularly impressed the crews of colliers and trading vessels sailing along the east coast and into the Thames estuary. Roddam needed to man *Cornwall* before he could fulfil his orders to sail round to Spithead to form part of a squadron intended for the Mediterranean. In November 1777, when *Cornwall* was anchored in The Downs, Roddam acquired two seamen recently pressed from a Greenland whaler but their recruitment presented him with a difficult legal problem. Greenlanders were amongst those categories of seamen entitled to receive Admiralty protections from impressment.[26] Accordingly, on his arrival at Spithead, Roddam was served with two writs of *habeas corpus* demanding the seamen's release. He wrote to the port-admiral, Sir Thomas Pye:

> Having this minute been served with the enclosed writs I think it is my duty to transmit them to you for your directions how I am to proceed and further beg to inform you that they were taken out of a Greenland ship being found in actual mutiny not only resisting H.M. boats coming on board but had confined their captain having sentinels placed at the cabin door when the officers came on board.[27]

Roddam transferred the seamen to the flagship pending a decision from the Admiralty. A week later Roddam was informed that the writs 'had not been regularly issued' and that both seamen could be entered on *Cornwall*'s books 'to serve as part of her complement in the same manner as before'.[28]

As it turned out Roddam spent only a few more months as captain of *Cornwall*. In April 1778 he became Rear-Admiral of the White as part of a general round of promotions and was ordered back to Chatham, this time as the port-admiral, where he remained until the end of the American War. Thereafter Roddam returned to his estates in Northumberland to consolidate the improvements he had begun 20 years before. Together with his brother William, he devoted much of his time to Roddam Hall and the parkland surrounding it. Admiral Roddam also took an interest in the career of his youngest brother, Collingwood Roddam, who was a captain in the East India Company.

In June 1786 a number of Whitby merchants, owners of *Chapman*, presented Roddam with a silver bowl as a token of their gratitude:

> For his active and kind assistance in getting the said ship from off the Isle of Sheppey where she was run ashore by the pilot in March 1783 on her voyage from Madras and for the various essential services he afforded them whilst in command of H.M. fleet at The Nore.[29]

It was also during this period that Roddam is reputed to have introduced Collingwood to his future wife Sarah daughter of John Erasmus Blackett. Roddam was distantly related to Sarah's mother and Collingwood's marriage in 1791 cemented these family ties and strengthened the Admiral's determination to use his influence on Collingwood's behalf. In October 1794 Admiral Bowyer wrote to Roddam:

> I write you this letter that I may not lose the satisfaction I always feel in doing justice to the merit of a friend of yours in saying that I do not know a more brave, capable or better officer in all respects than Captain Collingwood. I think him a fine character and I told Lord Chatham when he was at Portsmouth that if ever he had to look for a first captain to a commander-in-chief...he would not find a better than our friend Collingwood.[30]

As port-admiral at Portsmouth between 1789 and 1792 Roddam was regularly solicited to use his influence to secure the promotion of several young Northumbrian officers[31] but the death of his second wife, Alithea Calder, seems to have prompted his decision to strike his flag and return to his estates at Roddam. Thereafter he saw no further service although he appears to have volunteered for it on several occasions.

In September 1795 soon after his promotion to Admiral of the Red, Roddam married for a third time. His wife, Ann Harrison, was co-heiress to her uncle George Colpitts of Killingworth Hall, a Newcastle merchant and coal owner. Despite his age Roddam possessed, according to one contemporary biographer, '…a strength of constitution equal to the activity of his mind',[32] and he continued to enjoy the benefits of his wealth and status in provincial society. He regularly attended quarter sessions in his capacity as a magistrate and continued to oversee the management of his Roddam and Little Houghton estates. In May 1805 he was active in promoting the introduction of an alternative mail coach service between Newcastle and Edinburgh via Wooler and Kelso:

> As it certainly will be a very essential service and good to the centrical [sic] parts of Scotland and Northumberland being by many miles nearer and a very excellent turnpike road.[33]

The Admiral's penchant for entertainment and the social round of feasts and functions was well known although it occasionally got the better of him. In July 1801 in a letter to his father-in-law, Collingwood alluded to one of the consequences of Admiral Roddam's active social life:

> The poor Admiral I am afraid does not well recover from the accident that befell him in one of his sportive humours. He cannot yet walk but is taken into the air in a chair in fine weather.[34]

It was, perhaps, an accident waiting to happen and Roddam never fully recovered from the sprain. Nevertheless, he continued to take an active interest in the naval careers of his Northumbrian protégés. In 1803 he recommended William Landless to Collingwood and wrote to Nelson the following year urging him to promote Lieutenant MacKenzie who was then serving on the frigate *Hydra* [38].

He was vigorous in defence of his brother-in-law, Vice-Admiral Sir Robert Calder, after a court martial in December 1805 reprimanded him for '...not having renewed the engagement with the combined fleet and having not taken and destroyed all of the ships of the enemy'.[35] Calder's squadron had intercepted Villeneuve's fleet off Cape Finisterre in July 1805 after its return from the diversionary voyage to the West Indies. Calder's outnumbered squadron took two prizes during the initial engagement but his reluctance to renew the action on the following day was criticised at the Admiralty and he subsequently demanded a court martial to exonerate his decision. Unfortunately for Calder it was held at Portsmouth as the battered Trafalgar ships returned to England and in the context of Nelson's lying-in-state before the pomp and ceremony of his funeral. Roddam criticised the injustice of Calder's sentence and wrote to the *Naval Chronicle*:

> Sir Robert Calder saved us, and further, *he* and *he alone*, laid the entire foundation of every subsequent victory in this war; no victory off Cadiz, no victory in the West Indies etc. etc. No honours or rewards in consequence would have taken place *but for him* and yet this is the man Englishmen have been taught and permitted to abuse![36]

Service opinion eventually turned to Calder's support and he was later rehabilitated becoming Commander-in-Chief Plymouth and Vice-Admiral of the Blue in 1810. Roddam did not live to see his brother-in-law vindicated but his support for Calder and the injustice he felt about his mistreatment, was enshrined in his will:

> I give to the said Sir Robert Calder the sum of £1,000 and devise and bequest that these are so made by me as a mark of my high opinion of his service to his King and Country.[37]

Robert Roddam, Admiral of the Red, died at Killingworth on 31 March 1808, aged 88. He was buried in the family mausoleum at Ilderton the following week. As the last member of the male line of Roddam his estate passed to William Stanhope, a distant relative, on condition that:

> He take the name Roddam within a year of my death and keep my mansion house at Roddam with the office, gardens, pleasure grounds and plantations thereunto belonging and also the farmhouses and other buildings upon my estates in complete repair and condition.[38]

Roddam made cash bequests of almost £7,000 to various friends and relatives as well as leaving £500 to his servants. Collingwood received the news of the Admiral's death several months later. A contemporary observer wrote:

> During a long and active life, he has ever been the sailor's friend. No sailor's widow, or orphan, ever sued to him without receiving his benevolent assistance and such was his well known attachment to hospitality and benevolence that his table was always ready to receive his brother officers of all descriptions and every other person fit to be placed at it.[39]

References

1. Hughes, E., *North Country Life in the Eighteenth Century*, Oxford University Press (OUP) (1952), p. 113.

2. Newcastle Central Library (NCL), *Public Characters of 1802-03*, anon., [n.pub.] [n.d.], p. 132.

3. Clayton, T., *Tars*, Hodder & Stoughton (2007), p. 48.

4. Rodger, N.A.M., *The Wooden World: an Anatomy of the Georgian Navy*, Collins (1985), p. 281.

5. Admiral Phillip Cavendish to Admiralty, 7 October 1740. See Rodger, N.A.M., *The Command of the Ocean*, Penguin Books (2005), p. 322.

6. Rodger, *Command of the Ocean*, p. 322.

7. Augustus John Hervey (1724-1779), third Earl of Bristol, was one of the most colourful and successful naval commanders of his day, serving with distinction throughout the War of Austrian Succession and the Seven Years War.

   'His private life was marked by extravagant infidelities, his professional career by daring brilliance, his personal and private opinions by unbridled passion.'

   (Rodger, N.A.M., *The Wooden World*, p. 302).

8. NCL, *Public Characters*, p. 135.

9. National Maritime Museum (NMM), LBK 29, Admiralty to Commander Robert Roddam, 1 January 1747.

10. NMM, LBK 29, de Lancey to Captain Robert Roddam, 12 June 1750.

11. NMM, LBK 29, de Lancey to Captain Robert Roddam, 20 June 1750.

12. NMM, LBK 29, Admiralty to Sir George Clinton, Governor of New York, 4 December 1750.

13. The National Archives (TNA), ADM 51/4205, Log of H.M. Ship *Greenwich*, 23 August 1756.

14. TNA, ADM 51/4205, 20 December 1756.

15. TNA, ADM 51/4205, 5 January 1757.

16. NMM, ROD/2, Rear-Admiral Hon. George Townsend to Captain Robert Roddam, 29 January 1757.

17.   NMM, Minutes of the Court Martial of Captain Robert Roddam held on board *Marlborough* at Port Royal, Jamaica, 14 July 1757.

18.   NMM, Minutes of the Court Martial of Captain Robert Roddam.

19.   Clayton, *Tars*, p. 109.

20.   *Tars*, p. 126.

21.   *Tars*, p. 126.

22.   NCL, *Public Characters*, p. 144.

23.   Ordnance Survey Explorer Sheet 332, GR 023203.

24.   *Newcastle Courant*, 23 March 1816.

25.   Northumberland Record Office (NRO), Sant/Beq/18/2/1, p. 221.

26.   For a full discussion of the background and potential consequences of impressing Greenland seamen, see Barrow, T., The Noble Ann Affair 1779, *Press Gangs and Privateers: Aspects of the Maritime History of North East England 1760-1815*, Bewick Press (1993), pp. 13-22.

27.   NRO, 632/A/Box 1, Captain Robert Roddam to Admiral Sir Thomas Pye, 3 December 1777.

28.   NRO, 632/A/Box 1, Admiral Sir Thomas Pye to Captain Robert Roddam, 9 December 1777.

29.   *Newcastle Courant*, 24 June 1786.

30.   NRO, 632/A/1-8, Admiral Sir George Bowyer to Admiral Robert Roddam, 11 October 1794. Collingwood had distinguished himself as a flag-captain to Bowyer in *Barfleur* at the Battle of the Glorious First of June. Admiral Bowyer lost his leg in the action and wrote to Roddam from his convalescence at Cowes on the Isle of Wight.

31.   Roddam continued to use his considerable influence to support Collingwood and promote the naval careers of other Northumbrian naval officers such as Lieutenant William Landless who served briefly under Roddam in 1792 and later under Collingwood.

32.   NCL, *Public Characters*, p. 150.

33.   The letter was written on Admiral Roddam's behalf by his wife Ann Roddam to Robert Trotter, Postmaster General at Edinburgh, 24 May 1805.

      http://www.victorianweb.org/previctorian/letters/trotter.html

34.   NRO, ZBL228, Admiral Collingwood to J.E. Blackett, 4 July 1801.

35.   *Newcastle Courant*, 4 January 1806.

36.   *Naval Chronicle*, Vol. 27, p. 451, cited in Tracey, N., *Who's Who in Nelson's Navy*, Chatham Publishing (2006), p. 69.

37.   NRO, 5935/10, Will of Admiral Roddam, 5 September 1807.

38.   Will of Admiral Roddam.

39.   NCL, *Public Characters*, p. 15.

'I have a gentleman from Newcastle for my captain but he is a man of no talent as a sea officer and of very little assistance to me, so that the full weight of everything lays on me.'

[Admiral Collingwood to Edward Collingwood
23 September 1805]

Collingwood's Captain

Edward Rotheram 1753-1830

Few of Collingwood's officers attracted more invective and acerbic wit from the Admiral's pen than Edward Rotheram, who served as his flag-captain in *Dreadnought* [98] and *Royal Sovereign* [100] in 1804-05. Indeed, such was the extent of Collingwood's contempt for Rotheram that it even came to the notice of Lord Nelson who famously attempted to reconcile their differences before the Battle of Trafalgar, or so the story goes. Inevitably, there is no simple explanation for the troubled relationship between them. Despite the length of their respective naval careers, Rotheram and Collingwood served together for less than a year. There was no pre-history of earlier, negative encounters between them and Rotheram's links with Newcastle might have been expected to have softened Collingwood's attitude towards him and smoothed their troubled relationship. Was it because Rotheram had been appointed to *Dreadnought* without Collingwood's knowledge or was it simply a conflict of temperament and personality, not uncommon in the crowded and confined quarters of a large warship at sea?

Rotheram was clearly a cantankerous character and a poor man-manager, protective of his authority and quick to take offence at those who appeared to threaten it. His sea-going career is littered with examples of acrimonious disputes with other officers and it ended in 1808, a year after a court martial reprimanded him for 'unofficerlike conduct' when captain of *Bellerophon* [74]. At the same time few officers, including Collingwood himself, questioned Rotheram's courage or experience. As acting lieutenant of *Monarch* [74] he took part in Rear-Admiral Sir Samuel Hood's indecisive engagements against the French fleet off Martinique and the Chesapeake Capes in 1781 as well as Rodney's victory at the Battle of the Saintes (9-12 April 1782). Later, as first lieutenant of *Culloden* [74] at the Battle of the Glorious First of June, Rotheram was favourably noticed for his actions in boarding the battered and sinking *Le Vengeur* [74] and arranging for the evacuation of her captain and over 100 of her crew before she foundered. It seems unlikely that Collingwood, who also fought at that battle, did not hear of Rotheram's exploits.

Edward Rotheram was born at Hexham in Northumberland in 1753. His father, John Rotheram, studied medicine at the University of Edinburgh and set up in practice at Hexham before moving to Newcastle in 1760 where he established a reputation for literature and science. He became physician to Newcastle Infirmary in 1771 and was amongst the founding members of Newcastle Literary and Philosophical Society. Edward's elder brother John was a student of the famous botanist Carl Linnaeus (1707-1778) and later became Professor of Natural Philosophy at St. Andrews University between 1795 and 1804. Edward himself appears to have exhibited considerable mathematical ability under the tutelage of the celebrated Dr. Charles Hutton and, according to one author, '…evinced a marked preference for navigation'.[1]

In 1770 Rotheram was apprenticed to a master in the coal trade and spent seven years amongst the collier seamen of the Tyne and Wear. They were a rough and sometimes violent fraternity of mariners and it was here that Rotheram seems to have acquired some of the bad habits in the management of men that Collingwood so disapproved of. Without seeming to know much about his background, Collingwood considered that Rotheram had '…the stile [sic] of the coal trade about him', almost certainly a reference to Rotheram's abrasive manner and occasional use of intemperate language. He asked if Rotheram had been brought up in the Navy and disparaged his captain's nautical competence.[2]

Despite these withering criticisms, it appears that Rotheram had gained sufficient experience to assume command of a collier when, like James Cook before him, he decided to throw it up and join the Royal Navy. He was entered onto the books of *Centaur* [74] as an able seaman in April 1777, becoming a midshipman and then a master's mate in a relatively short time. It was during this period that he gained his first experience of a fleet action when *Centaur*, as part of Admiral Keppel's fleet, was involved in the indecisive battle off Ushant in July 1779. In October 1780 Rotheram was promoted acting lieutenant of *Monarch* then part of a squadron of warships sent to reinforce Admiral Rodney's fleet in the West Indies. Subsequently, part of this squadron, six ships of the line commanded by Rear-Admiral Sir Samuel Hood in *Barfleur*, formed the rear division of Admiral Graves' fleet in the crucial battle off the Chesapeake in September 1781. It was the decisive turning point of the American War of Independence. A confusion of signals between Graves and Hood contributed to the failure of the British fleet to inflict a decisive defeat on their French opponents and prevent them from returning to the Chesapeake and blockading Cornwallis' army at Yorktown several days later. 'It was said by some contemporary critics that the direct outcome of the engagement was the loss of the American Colonies', a view that has remained largely unchallenged ever since. Some maritime historians, notably Kenneth Breen and Nicholas Rodger, have indicted Hood's failure to support Graves and questioned the former's version of events which sought to deflect attention from his own failures and put the blame on Graves.[3]

Monarch and Hood acquitted themselves rather better the following year during the engagements with de Grasse's fleet off Dominica and the Iles de Saintes on 9 and 12 April 1782.

The Battle of the Saintes is famously associated with 'the breaking of the line' a tactic later used so effectively by Nelson at Trafalgar. Whether this was the product of chance or deliberate strategy on the part of the British commander, Admiral Sir George Rodney, remains a matter of dispute. During the morning phase of the day-long battle on 12 April *Monarch* took her station immediately astern of Rear-Admiral Hood's flagship *Barfleur* and engaged ships of the French rear for two hours. By 11 a.m. both vessels passed out of range and since the early breeze had disappeared to a flat calm, Captain Reynolds ordered *Monarch*'s boats to pull the ship round on to a reciprocal heading so that he could rejoin the battle. Early in the afternoon, however, *Monarch* was forced to break off the action once again having expended her powder. Nevertheless, with replenishment of 40 barrels of powder from the frigates *Flora* [36] and *Andromache* [32], Reynolds succeeded in getting his ship back into action late in the afternoon although by that time the battle was won.[4]

As an acting lieutenant Rotheram was responsible for directing a battery of guns on *Monarch*'s lower deck where he must have witnessed the grisly consequences of French shot on the seamen who fought there. British casualties sustained in the actions of

9 and 12 April were 261 killed and 837 wounded. *Monarch's* losses, 16 killed and 33 wounded, were amongst the highest suffered by an individual ship in the British fleet, most of them inflicted during the morning phase of the Saintes battle. Rotheram was unscathed and his promotion to lieutenant was confirmed on 19 April 1783 soon after *Monarch* returned to England. He must have been disappointed that it did not immediately lead to further employment.

The end of the American War provoked a rapid demobilisation of the fleet and hundreds of newly promoted officers like Rotheram were forced to live on half pay until they could secure another sea-going commission. He returned to his father's house in Westgate Road, Newcastle, where he spent most of the following four years. It turned out to be the longest period of unemployment during his active naval career. At the same time it provided him with opportunities to visit the Assembly Rooms and engage in the social life of the town. In March 1785 Rotheram married Dorothy Harle daughter of the jailer of Newgate prison in Newcastle. The couple initially set up home in the town but two years later, according to his own account, '…having attended daily at the Admiralty for three years', he was commissioned as fifth lieutenant of *Bombay Castle* [74] and instructed to join the ship at Plymouth. An account of the expenses he incurred is often used by naval historians to demonstrate the hidden costs of a naval officer fulfilling a new commission.

The purchase of equipment such as a telescope, navigational instruments, sword and speaking trumpet, together with tropical clothing and his contribution to wardroom expenses, brought his total outlay to over £90, considerably more than his annual salary of £72. Rotheram complained:

This good officer hath served one whole year in defence of his King and country, his clothes worn out and stock exhausted, finds himself in debt to the amount £18-17s-10½d.[5]

Exact expenses of a lieutenant who lived near three hundred miles north of London and received orders to join his ship at Plymouth			
	£	s	d
From his house to London	13	7	7½
From London to Plymouth	4	4	6
Two weeks board and lodging at Plymouth	2	0	0
Fees for taking up a commission	1	1	0
Cost of a uniform, gold-laced hat, Great coat, 14 shirts, 12 pairs stockings, 6 pairs shoes, 1 pair boots	7	15	0
Cash	5	5	0

Source: NMM SPB/15.

In April 1788 he was appointed to *Culloden*, Captain Sir Thomas Rich, whom he followed into *Vengeance* [74] in 1790 before finally returning to *Culloden* as first lieutenant in December 1792. Rotheram's re-appointment to *Culloden* proved to be a turning point in his naval career.

Under the command of Captain Isaac Schomberg *Culloden* formed part of the second division of Admiral Lord Howe's fleet at the Battle of the Glorious First of June in 1794. Amongst *Culloden*'s consorts that day were Collingwood's *Barfleur* and Gambier's *Defence* [74] whose part in the final and decisive phase of the battle became the stuff of legend and the subject of a famous painting now in the National Maritime Museum, Greenwich. *Culloden* took little part in the early encounters with the French fleet or in the skirmishes of 31 May, '…the day of fog and waiting'[6] but during the main action of 1 June she engaged *Le Tyrannicide* [74] and then the larger *Le Republicaine* [110] which had been badly damaged by several British ships earlier in the action. Towards the end of the battle Schomberg attempted to take possession of one of them as a prize but *Culloden* was recalled[7] to form a reserve around Howe's flagship and the French ships were able to escape. *Culloden*'s final duty was to take possession of the wreck of *Le Vengeur* and in doing so Rotheram attracted favourable attention to himself. The duel between *Brunswick* [74] and *Le Vengeur* was '…one of the epics of the sailing navy' and the subject of several paintings of the battle.[8] The two ships battered each other at point blank range for over four hours before the French captain surrendered, his ship totally dismasted and in a sinking condition. Many years later the fourth lieutenant of *Culloden* provided an eyewitness account of the events that followed.

> The *Vengeur* totally dismasted, going off before the wind, her colours down, Lieutenant Richard Deschamps, fourth of the *Alfred* [74], took possession of her. The next man on board was the *Culloden*'s Lieutenant Rotheram. Deschamps went up the side and Rotheram got in at the lower deck port, saw that the ship was sinking and went to the quarterdeck. I am not positive which boat got first on board. Rotheram returned with Captain Renaudin and his son and one man and reported her state whereupon other boats were sent. I heard him personally report to Captain Schomberg the *Vengeur*'s state: That he could not place a foot rule in any direction, he thought, that would not touch two shot holes.[9]

Rotheram returned to the wreck of *Le Vengeur* and organised a rapid evacuation of some of the survivors before the ship rolled on to her beam ends and sank. In recognition of his prompt action and as a senior lieutenant of a ship of the line Rotheram was promoted commander in July 1794. He left *Culloden* soon afterwards. Later, but under another captain, Thomas Troubridge, the ship's company staged a mutiny in protest at the poor condition of the ship. They were eventually persuaded to return to their duty after receiving assurances of an amnesty, but ten of the ringleaders were subsequently arrested and tried before a court martial; two were acquitted and three pardoned but the other five were hanged. The duplicity of the naval captains associated with the suppression of the *Culloden* mutiny embittered naval seamen everywhere and it was later used by Valentine Joyce during the Spithead Mutiny to remind them of the need to be suspicious of empty promises.[10]

Following his promotion Rotheram was commissioned to command *Camel*, ex-*Mediator* [44], converted to an armed store ship and attached to the Mediterranean Fleet. Ironically, she was one and the same ship that Collingwood had commanded in the West Indies ten years before. It was during this period that the earliest evidence of Rotheram's administrative inadequacies and tendency to draw unfavourable attention to himself first emerged.

In 1802 he received several letters from the Navy Board asking him to account for the delivery of 'a quantity of slops', principally shirts and shoes, sent by orders of Admiral Sir John Jervis from Leghorn to Gibraltar in February 1796. The stores had gone missing at Gibraltar and the consigning merchants, Messrs. Littledale and Broderick had clearly not been paid for them. Rotheram, by then a post-captain commanding the frigate *Lapwing* [28], considered his case 'a confounded hard one'. He claimed to have no recollection of the transaction despite:

… receiving a copy of a receipt alleged to be signed by me although I am not conscious of having signed such receipt or receiving a lading for such stores.

Whether he was successful in his attempts to resolve the fate of the missing stores and avoid a payment of over £500 to the Navy Board remains unrecorded, in Rotheram's correspondence at least. It seems likely that he was a victim of the embezzlement and corruption endemic in government administration at that time. Rotheram later discovered that '…the person who was the store keeper at Gibraltar has been turned out of his place long ago for improper conduct'.[11]

After a few months in command of *Camilla* [20] in the English Channel during 1797 Rotheram was commissioned to *Hawke* [16], sloop of war, and sailed for the West Indies the following year. Based regularly at Fort Royal, Martinique, sailing routine patrols for convoy protection and intelligence gathering, Rotheram visited Tobago, St. George's Bay in Grenada and English Harbour in Antigua, all of them familiar to naval officers of Collingwood's generation. In June 1799, off Guadeloupe, he captured

… a Spanish brig called *Lastres Felicidades*, Domingo Dages master, mounting 6 six pounders and twenty three men from Malaga bound to Vera Cruz laden with dry goods and wine and had been out thirty three days.[12]

The West Indies was one of the most unhealthy stations frequented by British warships in this period and there was a good deal of sickness amongst the crew. While *Hawke* was refitting at English Harbour one man died, others reported sick, and several seamen attempted to desert. Then, in April 1800, Rotheram wrote the first of three letters to Lord Hugh Seymour, Commander-in-Chief West Indies, requesting him to convene courts martial to try three of *Hawke's* officers for insubordination and neglect of duty. They represent the earliest evidence of Rotheram's failure to sustain effective working relationships with his junior officers. In the first letter he wrote:

> On 18th February last in the evening H.M. sloop *Hawke* under my command then being at sea I thought proper to reef the topsails a little before sunset and ordered the hands to be turned up for the purpose and observing the officers did not come up at the same time according to the established orders of the ship I thought fit to reprimand Lieutenant Wools for his neglectful conduct when he turned his back on me when going down the quarterdeck ladder in a most contemptuous manner saying he came up as soon as he was called…and my calling him again and desiring him not to be insolent he in a most disrespectful and contemptuous manner said to give me none of your insolence Sir on which I immediately ordered him into his cabin…. I have therefore to request your Lordship will be pleased to order a Court Martial to try the said Lieutenant Wools for disobedience of orders, neglect of duty and contempt for me his commander in the execution of my office.[13]

Two further letters, both written on the same day, requested courts martial on William Lucas, the master, and Thomas Goodchild, Sergeant of Marines, for drunkenness and contempt. Lucas was contrite and subsequently wrote a letter of apology to Rotheram which induced him to withdraw his request for a court martial but those on Wools and Goodchild went ahead. Rotheram's correspondence alluded to Wools '…having been tried on similar charges and reprimanded by court martial before'. Incidents such as these subsequently occurred with monotonous regularity and were clearly the result of Rotheram's irascible temperament which drew him into disputes with his subordinates that other, more thoughtful, less quick-tempered officers were able to avoid. He demanded respect but he did not inspire it and was quick to find fault in others or blame them for his own shortcomings.

Rotheram made a habit of complaining. Soon after his appointment as post-captain of *Lapwing* he wrote to Vice-Admiral Graeme at Chatham about the 'neglect of the Ordnance Department at this place', 'the inferior quality of the paint laid upon the guns' and 'the utmost contempt, indifference and defiance' with which the storekeeper handled his complaints.[14] During the summer of 1801 *Lapwing* was employed on routine patrols in the English Channel and spent some time in attendance on the Prince of Wales during one of his regular visits to the Brighton Pavilion. While engaged on this duty *Lapwing* ran aground on the Royal Sovereign Shoal. George Vernon Jackson, then a 14-year-old midshipman, later a Victorian admiral, remembered with amusement how '...40-50 women who were on board exerted themselves at the ropes in hauling the frigate from the Shoal'.[15] Later in his career, when captain of *Bellerophon*, Rotheram refused to allow his lieutenants to have their wives on board when the ship was anchored at Plymouth, which suggests a measure of inconsistency in his attitude to the practice. It was, perhaps, this inconsistency that contributed to Rotheram's troubled relationships with his officers. In August 1801 Rotheram wrote to the Admiralty requesting yet another court martial this time to try Lieutenant George Baker for breaches of the Articles of War.

> For having on the night of the 16th July quitted the deck in his watch between the hours of nine and ten at which time it was very bad weather and the ship very near the French coast...and upon investigating the case I find that Lieutenant George Baker repeatedly has left the deck in his watch....[16]

Lapwing returned to the Channel Islands in late October 1801 and was fortunate to survive a week of severe gales soon after her arrival there. Rotheram's seamanship certainly prevented the loss of *Renard* [18] one of two sloops of war that parted from their anchors during the storms. Unfortunately he was unable to save *William and Lucy*, a gun barge, and two merchant ships which were driven onshore and wrecked '…the night being so dark and boisterous I could make no observations but that of attending to the safety of my own ship in one of the hardest gales I ever experienced.'[17]

Lapwing was taken into dock and fully surveyed at Plymouth in December 1801 after sustaining further damage during a stormy passage from Guernsey. Rotheram reported the quarter gallery, some of the sash frames and stern windows defective and the main shrouds, chain plates and coppering in need of repair. *Lapwing* was still refitting at Plymouth in March 1802 when the port-admiral, Sir Thomas Pasley, received a letter from the Duke of Clarence requesting an explanation for Rotheram's refusal to provide a certificate of competence to a midshipman. The young man concerned, a Mr. T. Tildersley, clearly benefited from the patronage of royalty but was unable to proceed to his lieutenant's examination without it. Rotheram's letter to the Duke described a number of misdemeanours, including the loss of *Lapwing*'s boat, which he ascribed to Tildersley's irresponsibility and disobedience. 'I would not have acted justifiably to the service', he wrote, 'by signing a certificate for a young man whose merits did not entitle him thereto', and lamented, 'that a young man who aspires to the honour of your Royal Highness' patronage should so far forget himself.'

Notwithstanding his criticisms of Tildersley's competence, Rotheram was well aware of the likely consequences for his own career by denying the Duke's request. His letter continued:

Yet out of the respect and esteem I must ever have for your Royal Highness and it should be your opinion that the young man in question will do any credit to the service I will feel happy in meeting your Royal Highness' wishes upon this and every other occasion.[18]

Rotheram's letter represents a potent reminder of the power of patronage in Georgian society. Few sensible officers ignored it, especially when it was exercised at the highest level, and most were obliged to cultivate it for the sake of their own careers. *Lapwing* paid off after the Peace of Amiens and Rotheram, once again, found himself on half pay without a ship. It was more than two years before his own aristocratic connections finally succeeded in finding him another.

Rotheram appears to have benefited from the patronage of Francis, Lord Elcho (1749-1808) who was probably a friend of his brother John. Amongst the correspondence of Earl St. Vincent, First Lord of the Admiralty between 1802 and 1804, there is a letter to Lord Elcho expressing his disappointment that he was unable neither to find a ship for Rotheram nor 'encourage an immediate expectation of one'. St. Vincent acknowledged that Rotheram was 'an officer of merit' and reassured Lord Elcho that 'the interest your lordship takes in his fortunes will incline me to give him employment when I can do it consistently with prior engagements'.[19]

Rotheram was obliged to wait another year before the Admiralty found him a ship but it was a plum appointment, as flag-captain to an admiral. He joined *Dreadnought* at Plymouth in December 1804 and so began his brief and troubled relationship with Collingwood. *Dreadnought* was a relatively new ship built at Portsmouth and launched in 1801. After a short refit she sailed from Plymouth in January 1805 with orders to rejoin Admiral Cornwallis off Brest. The first hint of Collingwood's dissatisfaction with his flag-captain came in a letter to Erasmus Blackett:

...my captain has been laid up with the gout ever since
we came out so that I am forced to fag and without
Clavell, [Collingwood's first lieutenant] I should be very
ill off.[20]

By coincidence, the same day that Collingwood wrote these
words to his father-in-law, Villeneuve's Toulon Fleet passed
through the Straits of Gibraltar and arrived off Cadiz where
Admiral Sir John Orde's squadron of six ships of the line lay at
anchor. Outnumbered and unprepared, Orde withdrew to the
south rather than risk a battle and, believing that Villeneuve's fleet
was ultimately intended as a covering force for Napoleon's planned
invasion, decided to sail north to reinforce the Channel Fleet.

Dreadnought was off Cape Finisterre when news of Nelson's
pursuit of the French fleet to the West Indies arrived. Initially
Collingwood was expected to detach some of his ships to support
Nelson's squadron but he hesitated, unconvinced as to the real
purpose of Villeneuve's mission.

'I think it not improbable', he wrote to Alexander
Carlyle in Edinburgh, 'that I shall have those fellows
coming from the West Indies again...for this Bonaparte
has as many tricks as a monkey. I believe their object in
the West Indies to be less conquest than to draw our
forces from home'.[21]

It was a shrewd assessment of a developing situation and
persuaded him to sail for Cadiz where he knew there were Spanish
warships preparing to join the French fleet. Intelligence was the
key to an effective strategy and re-establishing a blockade of Cadiz
was the best way to obtain it. Initially he only had three ships and
a frigate to observe the preparations of the Spanish fleet but
Dreadnought's 98 guns represented a formidable floating battery
and Collingwood is reputed to have trained her seamen to fire
three rounds in five minutes. Unfortunately the advantages to be

gained from this unprecedented rate of fire were offset by *Dreadnought's* notorious reputation as a slow and cumbersome sailer that '…could never keep up with a fleet in a chase'.[22]

By contrast the other ships in Collingwood's squadron, *Achille* [74] and the recently commissioned *Colossus* [74], were faster and more manoeuvrable than the flagship. It was just as well, on 20 August Villeneuve's combined fleet appeared on the western horizon steering for Cadiz. Collingwood, hopelessly outnumbered just as Orde had been several months before, retreated slowly towards Gibraltar. Villeneuve detached 16 ships in pursuit. Collingwood shortened sail, tacked and stood towards them as if to give battle. He ordered *Colossus*, the swiftest ship in his squadron, to close with the French and at the same time made signals to an imaginary fleet beyond the eastern horizon. It was the oldest trick in the book but sowed sufficient doubt in Villeneuve's mind for him to recall the chasing ships and bear up for Cadiz. Once in the harbour Collingwood resumed his blockade and the scene was set for Trafalgar.

It was during the final month leading up to the battle that Collingwood penned his damning criticisms of Rotheram whose abrasive manner and limited abilities of command clearly exasperated him to such an extent that it entirely compromised the relationship between them. 'I have a gentleman from Newcastle for my captain', he wrote to his cousin, Edward Collingwood, 'but he is a man of no talent as a sea officer and of very little assistance to me'.[23]

Collingwood's use of 'gentleman' to describe Rotheram was deliberately sarcastic since it implied a set of values and behaviours which Rotheram consistently failed to demonstrate. His comments reflected a frequently expressed theme of Collingwood's correspondence, the promotion of what he deemed to be unsuitable officers:

…the truth is, in this great extensive navy, we find a great many indolent, half-qualified people to which may be attributed most of the accidents that happened.[24]

Despite his long experience at sea and his mathematical ability, which Collingwood himself considered absolutely necessary to a successful naval officer, Rotheram seemed to have lacked both the initiative and quarterdeck behaviour that Collingwood expected of a 'gentleman'. His description of Rotheram as a 'stick' and his reference to him having 'the stile [sic] of the coal trade about him', point to his distaste for his captain's demeanour and methods of command. With hindsight, Collingwood's jaundiced view of Rotheram seemed entirely justified by the circumstances of his post-Trafalgar career.[25]

Given the extent of his dislike it might seem surprising that Collingwood decided to take Rotheram with him when he shifted his flag to *Royal Sovereign* a week before Trafalgar. His decision to do so reflected his own concern to act correctly and avoid placing personal prejudice before a sense of duty. By doing so Collingwood came to appreciate that Rotheram did possess some of the qualities he expected of a gentleman – bravery under fire and resourcefulness in a crisis.

The story of the Battle of Trafalgar and its aftermath is too well known to require a detailed treatment here. Suffice it to say that Rotheram behaved impeccably, famously refusing requests to remove a large and conspicuous gold-laced cocked hat on the grounds that: 'I have always fought in a cocked hat and I always will!'[26]

Royal Sovereign was the first ship into action, passing through the enemy's line close under the stern of *Santa Anna* [112], flagship of Vice-Admiral Ignacio Alava, about 12:15 p.m. Isolated and exposed to the gunfire of at least five enemy ships before support arrived, *Royal Sovereign* soon became an unmanageable wreck. At one point during the early stages of the battle only Collingwood and Rotheram remained on the quarterdeck. William Chalmers, the master, was almost cut in two by a cannonball while in conversation with the Admiral; James Clavell, the first lieutenant on whom Collingwood so much relied, was badly wounded and Collingwood himself bruised by a large splinter. Rotheram, resplendent in his gold-laced hat, was unscathed. After more than two hours of close-quarter action *Royal Sovereign*'s starboard broadside caused *Santa Anna*'s fore and mainmast to fall over the side. With her admiral dangerously wounded and almost half of her crew killed or injured she finally surrendered to *Royal Sovereign* and hauled down her colours.[27]

By this time *Royal Sovereign* had only her foremast left standing. George Castle, a young midshipman from Durham who left his own account of the battle, later recalled that 'she rolled so much after her masts were gone we could scarcely fight the lower deck, the water was almost knee deep.'[28]

On the news of Nelson's death, Collingwood assumed command of the British fleet. He shifted his flag into the frigate *Euryalus* [36] at the close of the battle leaving Rotheram with the unenviable task of repairing and preserving his battered warship. In rising winds *Royal Sovereign*, first under tow of *Neptune* [98] and then *Mars* [74], drifted dangerously close to the Trafalgar Shoals during the gales that followed the battle. On 25 October in winds gusting almost to hurricane force *Royal Sovereign*'s remaining mast collapsed under the strain and soon after the tow rope to *Mars* snapped. Without masts and the means to manoeuvre, drifting close to a lee shore, Rotheram's situation was critical. As her exhausted crew worked frantically during the night to rig a jury mast *Royal Sovereign* rolled deeply and laboured to respond to tempestuous seas. At one point a huge wave smashed through the stern gallery and into the cabin drenching the wounded men lying there. Rotheram, fearing the ship was about to run aground, took regular soundings. He later admitted that *Royal Sovereign* '...came 'very close to foundering...from shot holes and loss of masts'.[29] Fortunately, the wind moderated the following morning. With a jury mast rigged and a sail hoisted, *Royal Sovereign* made progress towards the British fleet and anchored close to them on Saturday afternoon. She finally reached Gibraltar on 2 November. George Castle lost no time in writing to his sister in Durham '...by the great mercy of God I am left safe and unhurt both from the enemy and the elements for I can safely say we have engaged both'.[30]

Royal Sovereign remained at Gibraltar for over two weeks but Collingwood gave Rotheram little opportunity for rest and recuperation. On 4 November, two days after his arrival, Rotheram was commissioned to command *Bellerophon* and sailed for England in company with *Belleisle* [74] and *Victory*, carrying the body of Lord Nelson.

Bellerophon had been in the thick of the fighting at Trafalgar and her captain, John Cooke, was killed early in the action. It fell to her first lieutenant, William Pryce Cumby to fight the ship through the battle and he did so heroically. Rotheram clearly recognised and respected the ability and achievement of his first lieutenant. Soon after *Bellerophon* arrived at Plymouth, he responded to the Admiralty's request to recommend any officers he considered worthy of promotion. On 17 December Rotheram replied:

> I have received your letter of 14th inst. informing me of their Lordships' intentions to promote the first lieutenants of the line of battle ships lately under the command of Vice-Admiral Lord Nelson in the action of 21st October last...in answer to which I have to acquaint you that Lieutenant Pryce Cumby was first lieutenant of the *Bellerophon* the whole of the action of 21st October, that he fought the ship some time after the captain was slain and I am well persuaded will merit any favour their Lordships may be pleased to bestow on him.[31]

Cumby left the ship, pending promotion, on Boxing Day 1805 and became a post-captain on 1 January 1806. Together with Rotheram he attended Nelson's state funeral later the same month. *Bellerophon's* battle damage was thoroughly repaired in the dockyard at Plymouth at a total cost of over £18,000, two thirds of which was expended on replacing masts, spars and rigging.[32] Her month-long refit offered Rotheram the opportunity to spend Christmas ashore at the family home in Stonehouse although this must have been tempered by the news that his eldest daughter, Katherine, had died during his absence a week after Trafalgar.[33]

Rotheram remained in command of *Bellerophon* until 1808 but, as Collingwood predicted, his methods and demeanour caused dissension among the officers and contributed to a decline in the discipline and efficiency of the crew. Each of *Bellerophon's* lieutenants had served under Cooke and Cumby and all of them found it difficult to adjust to Rotheram's oppressive manner. During her first spell of duty with the Channel Fleet in 1806 the first lieutenant, Edmund Thomas, detected a significant decline in the discipline of the crew:

> In the former part of my service in *Bellerophon* I have been in the habit of having my orders obeyed and seeing the orders of other officers obeyed when first issued but I now find that these are ignored when the men are in the tops.[34]

Thomas put it down to Rotheram's failure to support his lieutenants whenever they complained to him about the discipline of the men and his habit of reprimanding officers in front of the crew. Lieutenant Thomas recalled:

> Frequently after dinner, Captain Rotheram comes out of his cabin and abuses his officers when the duty of the ship is not done in that alert manner that it ought to be and which the general relaxation of discipline renders it utterly impossible it can be.[35]

The frequency with which Rotheram was obliged to report accidents and damage to *Bellerophon*'s masts and rigging was undoubtedly a consequence of ill-discipline amongst the crew. In September 1806 he was asked to account for the loss of two foretopmasts off Cape Finisterre. The first was the result of a lightning strike and clearly accidental but the second, which occurred just four days later, appears to have been preventable. Rotheram reported that the ship was close hauled in a light northerly breeze:

> When a sudden gust of wind laid her down and the foretopmast went over the side close above the cap. There were several ships of the squadron under the same sail as we were but none seemed to feel the violence of this vein of wind with the force that this ship did.[36]

Earl St. Vincent, commanding the Channel Fleet, blamed Rotheram's negligence and advised the Admiralty to charge the cost of the masts to Rotheram's wages.[37]

It is conceivable that the declining efficiency of *Bellerophon*'s crew derived from more than Rotheram's reluctance to support his officers in disciplinary matters. It may also have had something to do with his decision to collect information about individual members of the ship's company. Why he undertook to compile such a survey remains a mystery. One historian has suggested that it may have been a manifestation of Rotheram's academic background and that it was undertaken in the spirit of scientific enquiry. It could be that his formative years in the coal trade led him to identify with the lives of some of the seamen he commanded. Alternatively, it might simply have been an exercise to relieve the boredom of constant patrols to blockade the Channel ports. As Collingwood put it:

> Nothing can be duller than this sort of cruising to watch a port – the ships dawdling after one another for months

together, every day the same object in sight…the bleak and barren rocks of Ushant.[38]

Whatever the reason, Rotheram's detailed survey represents his lasting legacy to naval historians of the Nelson era. He concentrated his attention on 387 seamen in the ship's company recording their age, height, physical appearance, position on board and place of abode as well as their background and nautical experience. He discovered that almost half of *Bellerophon's* crew (49 per cent) were English, another quarter Irish (24 per cent) and the majority of the rest Scottish (12 per cent) and Welsh (7 per cent). John Stewart, a quartermaster from Berwick with 11 years experience, William Ferguson, 'a trusty fellow' from North Shields who had served 13 years in the Royal Navy and Henry Freeman from Newcastle, both quarter gunners, were amongst the oldest members of the ship's company.[39] As petty officers they probably suffered the consequences of declining discipline as much as the commissioned officers did. Tensions in the wardroom finally came to a head in March 1807 when the second lieutenant, John Alexander Douglas, wrote to the Admiralty requesting a court martial on Rotheram for unofficerlike and oppressive conduct. Rotheram countered with his own request for a court martial to examine the conduct of his principal lieutenants, Douglas and Thomas.

Rotheram's court martial was held on board *Salvador del Mundo* [112], the receiving ship at Plymouth, on 17-18 April 1807. Amongst the officers presiding were John Loring, a former captain of *Bellerophon* and Captain John Conn who sailed *Royal Sovereign* out to Cadiz in 1805 and transferred into *Dreadnought*, Rotheram's old ship, when Collingwood shifted his flag a week before Trafalgar.

Lieutenant Thomas, who had served under Loring, was the first to give evidence against his captain and cited several incidents between himself and Rotheram that he deemed to be unofficerlike.

He testified that on one occasion:

> When on duty on the quarterdeck I did not perform
> my duty to Captain Rotheram's wish and in the presence
> of all hands on deck Captain Rotheram shook his fist
> in my face and told me that I was of no more use than
> a broomstick!

Rotheram, he said, had doubted his honesty; 'Damn your word
Sir, I won't take it', and accused him 'of always wanting to get the
poor men punished'. Questioned about Captain Rotheram's
demand that officers should be at their duty at all times Thomas
replied that his captain had declared he was determined to break
his officers and that 'there would be nothing but
uncomfortableness in the ship'.[40] These accusations were
corroborated by several subsequent witnesses, all of whom testified
that Rotheram had subjected them to similar treatment at one
time or another. *Bellerophon*'s fourth lieutenant, Edward Hartley,
who had served as a master's mate at Trafalgar and was wounded
during the battle, was another victim of Rotheram's outbursts.
The third lieutenant remembered 'Captain Rotheram shaking his
spyglass at Lieutenant Hartley in a violent passion' and Hartley's
own testimony confirmed the circumstances in which it had
occurred:

> I have had many occasions to complain to Captain
> Rotheram for men being off deck in their watch,
> drunkenness and neglect of duty of which I am sorry
> to say no notice was taken and which has been the
> instigation of reducing the ship's company from the
> highest state of discipline to an infamous state of
> insubordination.[41]

Hartley accused Rotheram of using obscene language, verbally
abusing both himself and the first lieutenant, publicly quarrelling
with his officers and threatening the ship's chaplain. His evidence,

that the discipline of *Bellerophon*'s crew had deteriorated under Rotheram's command, must have been given with particular conviction. Just over a year before, in December 1805, Rotheram had written to the Admiralty in support of Hartley's promotion describing him as '…a very deserving petty officer and from what I can learn from Lieutenant Cumby conducted himself at all times in a manner that strongly recommends him to your Lordships notice'.[42] Lieutenant Hartley's promotion left an opportunity for *Bellerophon*'s senior midshipman, John Franklin, to become master's mate. Many years later, in 1847, he lost his life during an ill-fated expedition to the Arctic in search of the North West Passage. Franklin offered no incriminating evidence against his captain at the court martial.

Rotheram conducted his own defence on the second day of the court martial. He called three witnesses to testify on his behalf, Captain Stephen Sandys of the Royal Marines, Thomas Jewell, the purser, and Alexander Whyte, the surgeon. Sandys believed that there had been a combination amongst the officers against Rotheram and put it down to:

> Some disagreement with Captain Rotheram on points of duty…and he not having wished some of the lieutenant's wives to remain constantly on board when we were in port. There did not appear to be cordiality between the captain and the officers.

This was confirmed by the purser who, when asked by the court if he was aware of a combination of the officers, replied:

> I have the impression on my mind that there has been a party formed against Captain Rotheram and a spirit hostile to some of those who dined with him as far back as 2 December 1805. When the ship arrived off the port of Plymouth the officers convened in the wardroom and proposed that Captain Rotheram should

not be invited to the wardroom table to dine in
consequence of Mr. Thomas not being asked by
Captain Rotheram to breakfast or to dine which I
understand was occasioned by some misunderstanding
in points of duty.[43]

The court martial decided there was sufficient evidence to find
Rotheram guilty of unofficerlike conduct and duly reprimanded
him for it. The charge of oppressive conduct was not proven but
Rotheram's reputation was fundamentally damaged by the whole
affair. Collingwood, out in the Mediterranean, was surprisingly
sympathetic when he heard the news and wrote from *Ocean* in
June 1807:

I am sorry to learn of poor Rotheram who, though I
think him a stupid man, I was in hope that he would
go on in the ship I put him in, which I believe was the
only chance of being in a ship.[44]

Rotheram remained in command of *Bellerophon* for a full year
after his court martial although accidents continued to follow him
around. In August 1807 *Bellerophon* again suffered considerable
damage to her masts and rigging as the result of a lightning strike
in which one man was killed and nine others wounded. In his
report to the Admiralty Rotheram described it as:

A violent explosion of electric fluid...the report [of
which] far surpassed that of the largest cannon I ever
heard and affected the hearing of many in the ship,
every part of which was enveloped in a thick smoke
attended with a strong sulphurous smell...the main
topgallant mast totally disappeared except the heel and
the yard; the maintopmast head to heel shivered into a
thousand pieces and the fore part of the mainmast was
ripped off and thirteen feet from the upper end of it
totally disappeared...the mizzen topmast split and

shivered to pieces and the whole of the mast above the poop much damaged.[45]

Bellerophon returned to Plymouth where she was docked and repaired at a cost of just over £8,000. In June 1808 after further patrols off Brittany and in the Bay of Biscay Rotheram was superseded in command of *Bellerophon* by Captain Samuel Warren.

Now aged 54 and with many young, newly promoted officers looking for a command, and an unenviable record of accidents and litigation, it marked the end of Rotheram's sea-going career although he continued to make a nuisance of himself for many years to come. With a sufficient annual income from his Trafalgar prize money and the half pay he received from the Admiralty, Rotheram appears to have enjoyed a comfortable retirement in Plymouth where he lived for most of the remainder of his life.[46] Embittered by his treatment in the distribution of honours in 1815, when a number of officers he considered less worthy than himself became Knights Commander of the Bath,[47] Rotheram was awarded the lesser honour of Companion of the Bath despite having '…the honour to command the *Royal Sovereign* who led the British Fleet to victory, a victory too well known by its splendour to require any comment'.[48] In the years that followed he complained regularly through the newspapers about naval administration and the rapid promotion of the sons of aristocratic families. In 1825 when *Royal Sovereign* was taken into dock at Plymouth for conversion to a prison hulk Rotheram was presented with:

> A piece of the quarterdeck and part of the quarterdeck beam taken from the spot where that officer chiefly remained during the battle of Trafalgar, for the purpose of being made into a piece of furniture.[49]

Rotheram was appointed as one of the captains of Greenwich Hospital in 1828. He died at Bildeston in Suffolk on 6 November

1830 and was buried in the churchyard there in an unmarked grave. Many years later, in November 1891, Vice-Admiral W.B. Woolcoombe and the editor of the *Army and Navy Gazette*, Captain C.N. Robinson R.N., placed an advertisement calling for subscriptions to defray the cost of placing a headstone over Rotheram's grave and a memorial to him on the south wall of the church close to the chancel arch. In July 1918 Cuthbert Eden Heath presented Lloyds with a large silver vase originally presented to Rotheram by Lloyds Patriotic Fund 'for his meritorious service in contributing to the signal victory obtained over the fleets of France and Spain off Cape Trafalgar, 21 October 1805'. The vase was one of 66 presented to the senior naval officers who fought at the battle. Only four of them survive.[50] The ultimate accolade and one that Rotheram undoubtedly would have approved of, was the launch, in March 1942, of the destroyer *H.M.S. Rotheram*. It represented the final act of rehabilitation of a naval officer whose reputation will be forever fixed by Collingwood's critical correspondence.

He was an irascible character, difficult to work with and clearly not a 'gentleman' by contemporary standards of speech and behaviour. Nevertheless, his battle honours and courage under fire impressed even Collingwood and drew admiration from a later generation of naval officers. Those who were close to him remembered his 'dryness of wit gained largely in point and effect by the Northumbrian burr in his articulation' and his determination to tilt at the windmills of the establishment. Those who served with him were probably inclined to Collingwood's view 'I cannot sufficiently recommend Captain Rotheram'.[51]

References

1. Welford, R., *Men of Mark Twixt Tyne and Tweed*, Vol. III. (Walter Scott, 1895).

2. Hughes, E., *The Private Correspondence of Admiral Lord Collingwood*. Admiral Collingwood to his sister, 26 August 1805.

3. See for example, Breen, K., Graves & Hood at the Chesapeake, *Mariners Mirror* 66, 1 February 1980, pp. 53-65 and Rodger, N.A.M., *The Command of the Ocean*, pp. 352-353.

4. The National Archives (TNA), ADM 51/609, Journal of the proceedings of H.M. ship *Monarch*, Francis Reynolds Esq. Commander.

5. National Maritime Museum (NMM), SBK/15. Rotheram's Commonplace Book offers the account anonymously although it clearly relates to his personal experience of joining *Bombay Castle*.

6. Warner, O., *The Glorious First of June*, Batsford (1961), p. 120.

7. Warner, *The Glorious First of June*, p. 121.

8. Warner, *The Glorious First of June*, p. 124.

9. Staniforth, Collingwood's Captain – Two Letters, *Archaeologia Aeliana 4th Series XLIII* (1965) citing Thomas Carlyle, 'Critical and Miscellaneous Essays', Vol. VI, (1869).

10. Dougan, J., *The Great Mutiny*, Andre Deutsch (1966), pp. 108-109.

11. NMM, LBK/38. Letters of 9 & 21 March 1802 to Charles Fowler in London and 16 May 1802 to E. Pownall, Naval storekeeper, Gibraltar.

12. NMM, LBK/38, Rotheram to CinC West Indies, 6 July 1799.

13. NMM, LBK/38, Rotheram to CinC West Indies, 27 April 1800.

14. NMM, LBK/38, Rotheram to Vice-Admiral Alexander Graeme, CinC Chatham, 26 December 1800.

15. Pope, D., *Life in Nelson's Navy*, Chatham Publishing (1997), p. 175.

16. NMM, LBK/38, Rotheram to Admiralty, 13 August 1801.

17. TNA, ADM 1/2404, Rotheram to Admiralty, 5 November 1801.

18. NMM, LBK/38 Rotheram to HRH Duke of Clarence, 6 March 1802.

19. Staniforth, Collingwood's Captain – Two Letters, pp. 309-310.

20.   Newnham Collingwood, G.L., *A Selection from the Public and Private Correspondence of Vice-Admiral Lord Collingwood, interspersed with Memoirs of his Life*, (1829), Admiral Collingwood to J.E. Blackett, 9 April 1805.

21.   Adams, M., *Admiral Collingwood*, Weidenfeld & Nicholson (2005), p. 196.

22.   Lavery, B., *Nelson's Fleet at Trafalgar*, NMM (2004), p. 137.

23.   Duffy, M. (ed.), *Naval Miscellany*, Vol. VI, Ashgate for the Navy Records Society (2003). Admiral Collingwood to Edward Collingwood, 23 September 1805.

24.   Newnham Collingwood, *Public and Private Correspondence*, Admiral Collingwood to J.E. Blackett, 8 April 1800.

25.   For a full discussion of the changing social and professional character of naval officers in this period see Rodger, N.A.M., Honour and Duty at Sea 1660-1815, *Bulletin of the Institute of Historical Research*, Vol. 75, November 2002.

26.   This incident is cited in many accounts of Trafalgar and originates from Marshall, J., *Royal Naval Biography*, Vol. II, Part I. (1824), p. 300.

27.   TNA, ADM 50/41, Admiral Collingwood's Journal.

28.   George Castle's Trafalgar Letter, Nelson Dispatch, Vol. 6, Part 8 (October 1998). See appendix.

29.   NMM, LBK 38., cited by Clayton, T. & Craig, P. *Trafalgar: the Men, the Battle, The Storm*, p. 327.

30.   George Castle's Trafalgar Letter.

31.   TNA, ADM 1/2408, Rotheram to the Admiralty, 17 December 1805.

32.   Cordingly, D., *Billy Ruffian: The Bellerophon and the Downfall of Napoleon*, Bloomsbury Paperbacks (2003), Appendix 1.

33.   NMM, SBK/15. p. 222.

34.   TNA, ADM 1/5380, Evidence of Lt. Edmund Fanning Thomas.

35.   Evidence of Lt. Edmund Fanning Thomas.

36.   NMM, LBK/38, Rotheram to Vice-Admiral Sir Charles Cotton, 18 September 1806.

37.   TNA, ADM 1/2408, Rotheram to the Admiralty, 30 October 1806.

38.   Cordingly, *Billy Ruffian*, p. 209 and Northumberland Record Office (NRO), ZBL 235, Admiral Collingwood to J.E. Blackett, 4 July 1801.

39. TNA, ADM 36/16498 and Cordingly, *Billy Ruffian*, p. 209.

40. Evidence of Lt. Edmund Fanning Thomas.

41. TNA, ADM 1/5380, Evidence of Lt. Edward Hartley.

42. TNA, ADM 1/2408, Rotheram to the Admiralty, 17 December 1805.

43. TNA, ADM 1/5380, Evidence of Captain Stephen Miles Sandys, Royal Marines and Thomas Jewell, purser.

44. Hughes, *Private Correspondence of Admiral Lord Collingwood*, Collingwood to his sister 1 June 1807.

45. NMM, LBK/38, Rotheram to Admiral de Courcy, 28 August 1807.

46. Rotheram received £973 in prize money as a Trafalgar captain and an additional parliamentary award of £2,389-7-6d making a total of over £3,362. His half pay as a post-captain of a third rate ship amounted to between £130-140 per annum. See Lavery, B., *Nelson's Navy: The Ships, Men and Organisation, 1793-1815*, Conway Maritime Press Ltd. (1989), Appendix to Part VI, p. 326.

47. Rotheram's Commonplace Book named eight officers whom he considered less worthy than himself including Sir John Colpoys who 'was never in an action in his life', Sir John Yorke who, according to Rotheram, 'never did anything but talk' and two captains, Richard Grindall and the Earl of Northesk who 'behaved notoriously ill in the Trafalgar action'.

48. Lavery, B., *Nelson's Fleet at Trafalgar*, p. 197.

49. *Newcastle Courant*, 23 July 1825.

50. Staniforth, F., Collingwood's Captain, p. 306 and http://www.jjhc.info/heathcuthbert1939.htm

51. Adams, M., *Admiral Collingwood: Nelson's Own Hero* and Staniforth, F., Collingwood's Captain, p. 312.

'Landless has taken an exceedingly good prize, a boat from La Vera Cruz, very small but laden with cochineal, indigo etc. which will give him more prize money than I have got since I came out, except for Trafalgar.'

[Admiral Collingwood to Lady Collingwood
20 December 1806]

Collingwood's Lieutenant

William Landless 1762-1826

The naval career of William Landless, variously spelt Landles or Landels and similarly pronounced is, perhaps, the most interesting and instructive of all of Collingwood's Northumbrians. He was a competent and hugely experienced officer whose naval service reveals the impact of some of the key influences on the career of an officer in the Georgian navy. During 30 years at sea Landless participated in several decisive historical events of that era. As a prisoner he witnessed the surrender of General Cornwallis at Yorktown and, following his release, took part in the last major naval engagement of the American Revolutionary War, the Battle of the Saintes. In 1786, not long after he had been commissioned as a lieutenant, Landless joined the East India Company and spent most of the following decade climbing through its marine officer ranks. At a point where an independent command of an East Indiaman looked likely he returned to the Royal Navy as a lieutenant. His reasons for doing so remain unclear but were unlikely to have been financial. Moreover, the interruption of his naval service during the intervening years compromised his seniority and prospects of rapid promotion. In June 1797 he was commissioned to *Inflexible* [64] the focus and 'incendiary ship' of the mutiny at The Nore and subsequently fought in *Dreadnought* at Trafalgar. Collingwood considered him a rather morose and uninspiring character '…a dull heavy man and all the good you can say of him is that there is no harm in him'.[1] At the same time he respected his loyalty as a follower and his long association with the patronage of Admiral Roddam who recommended him to Collingwood in 1803.

Landless was born at Easington near Belford in Northumberland in 1762. His father, George Landless (1730-1805), was of Scottish extraction and a tenant of Abraham Dixon of Belford Hall. His name appears in the earliest surviving rental rolls for 1766 and by 1780 he was farming 96 acres which included possession of a watermill and the disused Belford Cragg windmill.[2] There is a suggestion that George Landless and other members of the extended family settled at Ford, in north Northumberland, following the proscription of the clans after Culloden and that they had formally been MacGregors but this is to a large extent conjecture.[3] Numerous Landles(s) families were living in and around Berwick and the Borders from the late seventeenth century, so many in fact that the use of the double 's' in rendering the surname may have been a means of differentiation. About 1750 another William Landless, probably a brother of George, was a tenant of Sir John Hussey Delaval at Barmoor Mill, near Lowick. Later, during the 1760s, he entered into an agreement with Sir John to mine coal in the same district. Several members of a later generation, contemporaries of Lieutenant Landless and possibly his cousins, were shareholders in the Old Shipping Company at Berwick between 1802 and 1810.[4]

Landless first went to sea as an apprentice in the coal trade in 1777 but entered the Royal Navy at Leith the following year. There seems little doubt that his decision to do so was influenced by a connection with the Younghusband family who farmed at Elwick, near Belford, and were near neighbours of William's father. Lieutenant George Younghusband, election agent for Sir John Delaval, was the impress officer at Leith between 1777 and 1782. He seems to have used these positions and the influence they gave him on the young man's behalf. In May 1778 William Landless, then aged 16, was shipped off to Chatham where Admiral Roddam was the port-admiral. He was entered onto the books of *Conquestador* [60], the receiving ship anchored at The Nore and within a year Roddam sent him to *Richmond* [32], Captain Charles Hudson, a frigate fitting out for service on the American station.

Soon after her arrival in the American war zone, in March 1780, *Richmond* together with *Roebuck* [44], *Romulus* [44] and *Renown* [50], under the command of Vice-Admiral Marriot Arbuthnot, took part in the bombardment and capture of Charleston. Then, leaving General Cornwallis in command of British troops in the Carolinas, Arbuthnot returned to New York to counter the threat of a French expeditionary force with seven ships of the line that occupied Newport, Rhode Island, in July 1780. *Richmond* was not amongst the frigates that fought at the first Battle of the Chesapeake in March 1781 but she was involved in the strategically decisive second battle the following September. During August *Richmond*, together with *Medea* [28] and *Iris* [28], was ordered to patrol off the Delaware as part of a line of frigates detailed to gather intelligence and give early warning of the arrival of a large French fleet with troop reinforcements for General Washington's army in Virginia. On 30 August 1781 the French fleet duly arrived; 26 sail of the line and seven frigates under the command of the Comte de Grasse. They anchored in Lynnhaven Roads at the mouth of the Chesapeake the following day. De Grasse lost no time disembarking an army of over 3,000 troops which marched to join the siege operations before Yorktown. The preliminaries for the end game of the American Revolution were now in place.

Without clear intelligence but conscious of the imminent arrival of de Grasse, the British fleet of 19 ships of the line, seven frigates and a fireship under the overall command of Rear-Admiral Thomas Graves sailed from Long Island on 31 August. *Richmond* formed part of Rear-Admiral Hood's division which included *Monarch*, Edward Rotheram's ship. On the morning of 5 September *Solebay* [28], scouting ahead of the main fleet, made the signal for a fleet in the south west. In favourable wind and weather conditions the British fleet formed a line of battle as the French ships, caught by surprise, struggled to slip their anchors and put to sea.

What followed was an indecisive, running fight, in which Hood's division failed to become closely engaged with any units of the French fleet so that the leading ships bore the brunt of the fighting. As darkness fell Admiral Graves sent his frigates with orders for the British ships to extend the line and maintain contact with de Grasse during the night so that he might renew the battle the following day. His plan was compromised, however, by the discovery that six of his ships had sustained damage and were unable to keep their station. British casualties amounted to 90 killed and almost 250 wounded.[5] During the evening of 8 September, while both fleets were still in sight of each other, Captain Hudson received an order from Rear-Admiral Graves to proceed into the Chesapeake with dispatches for Lord Cornwallis. Graves recognised that it was a risky venture and ordered Captain Dawson of *Iris* to sail in company '…as I understand from Captain Duncan of the *Medea* that the enemy have a considerable force there'.[6] *Medea* and *Iris* had looked into Chesapeake Bay the day before and observed that the French fleet had buoyed their anchors in their haste to put to sea on 5 September. Cutting the buoys away was likely to cause serious problems should the French fleet attempt to return to them and this appears to have been the intention of the British frigates on their egress from the Chesapeake.

When *Richmond* left the fleet on the evening of 8 September, 'under a press of sail', Hudson estimated that Cape Henry was '…NW by W distant between 15 and 20 leagues'. In a northerly wind he beat up for the Cape and on the morning of 11 September Hudson saw a fleet of 27 or 28 sail ahead on the weather bow. *Richmond* closed with the rearmost ship of the strange fleet and flew recognition signals but they went unanswered and he drew his own conclusions. 'I immediately tacked and stood to the southward with all the sail I could set, as did *Iris*, supposing them to be the enemy.' Initially there seemed to be a good chance that both frigates would escape but sailing into shoal waters, close to the land and disadvantaged by a significant shift in the strength and direction of the wind, *Richmond* and *Iris* were cut off by the chasing French ships. Hudson's account continued:

> Having no sort of chance of escaping…the wind continuing to back against us, the headmost ship began to fire and throw her shot over us. At two o' clock finding our retreat to windward totally cut off…and the enemy's ships almost surrounding us and keeping up a continual fire by which the mainmast of the *Richmond* was considerably wounded, her rigging cut and her sails much torn, at three o' clock finding it impossible to escape I caused her colours to be struck to the *Bourgoyne* a French 74-gun ship which was close on boarding us. At this time we were about four leagues to the southward of Cape Henry.[7]

Landless, along with the crews of both frigates, was taken prisoner and sent ashore where he subsequently witnessed the aftermath of the fall of Yorktown and surrender of Lord Cornwallis. *Richmond's* principal officers, Captain Hudson and the first lieutenant, James Rogers, appear to have been given their parole soon after the loss of Yorktown for both men were back in England by March 1782 where a court martial, which included a young Horatio Nelson, exonerated Hudson of all blame in the loss of *Richmond*. Landless, together with other prisoners, was exchanged into *Convert* [32] for passage to English Harbour, Antigua, in February 1782. Here he was drafted to *Royal Oak* [74] which was refitting there. She later sailed to join the ships of Rear-Admiral Hood's division.

Landless arrived in the West Indies just as the military/naval situation there moved towards its final stage. On 7 April the French fleet under the Comte de Grasse put to sea from Martinique escorting a homeward bound convoy of over 100 merchantmen, but delays in organising such a large fleet of ships and getting them underway enabled Hood's van division of the British fleet to catch up with them off Dominica. Sending his merchant ships into Guadeloupe, de Grasse detached 15 ships to engage Hood's eight and Tuesday 9 April became '...a day of drifting ships and sporadic gunfire along the coast of Dominica'.[8] Several British ships, including *Royal Oak* which led the British ships into action, became dangerously exposed to the gunfire of superior numbers. *Royal Oak*, together with *Alfred* and *Montague* [74], suffered considerable damage to their masts and rigging. Captain Bayne of *Alfred* was killed and *Royal Oak's* first lieutenant was amongst eight men killed; 30 others were wounded. As a young, 20-year-old midshipman, Landless came through the action unscathed but his ship was disabled and forced to quit her place in the line to effect repairs. The following day, in response to an order from Admiral Rodney to redeploy his damaged ships to the rear of the British fleet, Hood reported:

Sea Piece with British Men-of-War
[Nicholas Pocock]

In a freshening southerly breeze two British frigates get under way, probably bound up river to Chatham or The Great Nore. The frigate on the right, in port quarter view, has hoisted a 'pilot jack' at the foretopgallant masthead while the crew of the other frigate, labour at the capstan weighing the anchor.
[Courtesy of Tyne Wear Archives and Museums]

N.º 7
LIEUTENANT

A Naval Lieutenant c.1799
[Thomas Rowlandson]
Collingwood's lieutenant William Landless (1762-1826) benefited from
the patronage of Admiral Roddam throughout his naval career. He joined
Collingwood in 1803, fought in *Dreadnought* at Trafalgar and was promoted to
Commander in 1806.
[National Maritime Museum]

Easington Farm House
William Landless purchased the farm at Easington about 1808. The farmhouse and steadings were built during the 1820s as part of his extensive improvements. He died here in January 1826.
[Author's Collection with permission of Iris and Tony Oates]

The Landless Family Tomb at Ford, Northumberland
Landless chose to be buried at Ford with his first wife, Mary (d.1795) and their son William (d.1800). Evidence perhaps, that there may be some truth in the suggestion that the family originally settled here following the proscription of the clans after Culloden.
[Author's Collection]

Passengers boarding a Man-of-War
[Attributed to J.W. Carmichael]

Collingwood's midshipmen, Granville Thompson and George Castle began their naval careers at Portsmouth in September 1803. They joined Collingwood on *Venerable*, cruising off Brest, later the same month.

[Courtesy of Tyne Wear Archives and Museums]

Collingwood's Midshipman: Granville Thompson (1788-1817)
Thompson probably sat for this portrait in 1812 when he returned briefly to
Newcastle for the first time since joining Collingwood in 1803. He died of yellow
fever in the Bahamas in September 1817.
[Courtesy of Tyne Wear Archives and Museum]

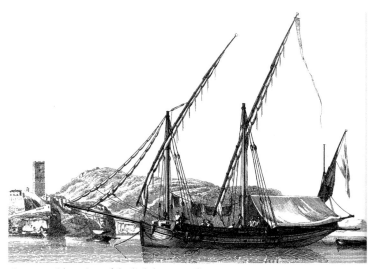

A settee with a view of the lighthouse at Genoa
[D. Serres, *Liber Nauticus* (1805)]
Common throughout the Western Mediterranean and the coast of North Africa.
Collingwood's lieutenant, William Landless, captured a similar vessel laden with
cochineal and indigo off the Algarve in December 1806. It proved to be a very rich prize.
[Courtesy of Tyne Wear Archives and Museum]

H.M. Sloop of War, Pelican
[D. Serres, *Liber Nauticus* (1805)]
Pelican was a similar vessel to *Scout* and *Kingfisher* in which Collingwood's
midshipman, Granville Thompson, served with distinction in the Mediterranean
between 1806 and 1811.
[Courtesy of Tyne Wear Archives and Museum]

His Majesty's Ship Amphion, off the Coast of Istria, August 8, 1809.

SIR,

I BEG Leave to inform you of a most gallant and successful Attack made by the Boats of this Ship and a Detachment of Seamen and Marines on the Enemy's Force at Cortelazzo, consisting of Six Gun Boats, and a Convoy of Merchant Trabaculos, moored in a strong Position under a Battery of Four Twenty-four Pounders, at the Mouth of the Piave, and in Sight of the Italian Squadron at Venice.

I had reconnoitred them on the 24th Instant, and found it impracticable, from the Shallowness of the Water, to get the Ship in, but I conceived they might be cut out by the Boats, provided I could carry the Battery; and this Opinion was confirmed by a Fisherman I detained the same Evening, who gave me a very correct Account of their Force and Situation: to prevent any Suspicion of my Design, I kept out of Sight of the Land till the Evening of the 26th, when I crowded all possible Sail, and we anchored off the Entrance of the Piave, at One on the Morning of the 27th. At Three a Detachment of Seamen and Marines, commanded by Lieutenant Phillott, First Lieutenant, assisted by Lieutenant Jones (2,) and Moore of the Marines, in all Seventy Men, were landed about a Mile below the Battery to the Southward, and advanced immediately to storm it, leaving Lieutenant Slaughter (Third Lieutenant) with the Command of the Boats, to push for the River before the Infant the Fort was carried: at a Quarter past Three the Alarm was given, the Attack was made the same Instant, and such Vigour in the Assault, that in Ten Minutes the Fort was completely in our Possession, and the concerted Signal made, the Guns were instantly turned on the Gun Boats, the Fire on which, and Musketry from the Marines, whom Lieutenant Moore had placed in a most excellent Situation, compelled them to instant Surrender; and our Boats took Possession of the Gun Boats and Vessels, as per enclosed List; Two of the former are of the largest Dimensions.

The Battery was a complete Work, with a Ditch, and Chevaux de Frize round it, and our Men entered it first by Scaling Ladders: the Commandant of the Fort made his Escape with some of his Men, Two were found dead, and One wounded, the rest, consisting of Sixteen of the 3d Regiment of Light Infantry, were made Prisoners. Having spiked the Guns, and totally destroyed the Battery and Barrack, the whole Detachment was reimbarked by One P.M.

I have now, Sir, the additional Pleasure of saying, that this Service was performed without the Loss of a Man on our Part. One Marine alone was wounded by an Explosion of Powder after we had Possession, but he is doing well.

The Gallantry and good Conduct of the Execution of this Attack, speaks for itself; I have only to say, he had the entire conducting of it, and on this, as on many other Occasions, fully justified the Confidence I placed in him. He speaks in the warmest Terms of Lieutenants Jones and Moore, and the Officers and Men under his Orders; the prompt Manner in which Lieutenant Jones turned the Guns on the Enemy's Vessels, and the judicious Disposition of the Marines by Lieutenant Moore, is highly Praise-worthy. In the Variety of Boat Service we have had, the Officers have particularly distinguished themselves, and some Months back were both severely wounded. The Silence and Regularity of the Seamen and Marines in their Advance to the Fort, and their Bravery in the Attack, is equally deserving of Praise, and truly characteristic of British Seamen. Inclosed is a List of the Officers and Midshipmen employed on Shore and in the Boats.

The Surrender of the Gun-Boats to the quick, that our Boats had not Time to join in the Attack on them, but were most actively employed afterwards in getting the Prizes out, under the Direction of Lieutenant Slaughter.—The above Vessels were taken at Cortelazzo for the express Purpose of protecting the Trade between Venice and Trieste, and were commanded by a Commandant de Division, Mons. Villeneuve, who is made Prisoner.

I have, &c.

(Signed) W. HOSTE, Captain.
Captain Hargood, His Majesty's Ship Northumberland, &c. &c. &c. in the Adriatic.

A List of Gun-Boats, &c. captured and destroyed by the Boats of His Majesty's Ship Amphion, W. Hoste, Esq; Captain, at Cortelazzo, on the 27th of August, 1809.

La Surveillante, Venetian Gun-Boat, commanded by Spiridione Augustino, Enseigne de Vaisseau, mounting One long Twenty-six-Pounder in the Bow, and 1 long Twelve-Pounder a-stern, with 4 Swivels mounted on the Gunwale, with a Complement of 36 Men, Copper bottomed and fastened, and quite new.

La Vedette, Venetian Gun-Boat, commanded by Aloise Tiozza, Lieutenant de Frégate, mounting 1 long Twenty-six-Pounder in the Bow, and 1 long Twelve-Pounder a-stern, with 4 Swivels mounted on the Gunwale, with a Complement of 36 Men, Copper-faltered.

No. 80, Venetian Gun-Boat, commanded by Giovanni Antonio, Alpirante (Midshipman), mounting 1 long Twenty-four-Pounder, with small Arms.

No. 76, Venetian Gun-Boat, commanded by Giovanni Villeneuve, Commandant de Division, mounting 1 long Twenty-four-Pounder, with small Arms.

No. 77, Venetian Gun-Boat, commanded by Andrew Moro, Alpirante, mounting 1 long Twenty-four-Pounder, with small Arms.

No. 64, Venetian Gun-Boat, commanded by Giovanni Marsâdo, Alpirante, mounting 1 long Twenty-four-Pounder, with small Arms.

Two Trabaceolos, laden with Rice, Cheese, &c.; taken.

Five Trabaceolos, laden with Wood and Charcoal; burnt in the River.

(Signed) W. HOSTE, Captain.

A List of Officers employed on Shore, and in the Boats of His Majesty's Ship Amphion, W. Hoste, Esq; Captain, at the Attack of the Enemy's Force at Cortelazzo, on the Morning of the 27th August, 1809.

C. G. R. Phillott, First Lieutenant.
G. M. Jones, Second Lieutenant.
William Slaughter, Third Lieutenant; in the Boats.
Thomas Moors, Lieutenant of Royal Marines.
J. Dalleny, Master's Mate.
Thomas Boardman, ditto.
Joseph Gape, Midshipman.
Charles H. Ross, ditto.
George Castle, ditto.
Charles Kempthorn, ditto.
William Lee Rees, ditto.
Charles Bruce, ditto.
Thomas Edward Hoste, Volunteer of the First Class.
F. G. Farewell, ditto.
Robert Spearman, ditto.
Jonathan Angas, Surgeon's Assistant.

(Signed) W. HOSTE, Captain.

An extract from the London Gazette describing the attack at Cortelazzo in 1809.

Capt. William Hoste's account of the cutting-out and capture of 6 Venetian gunboats by the boats of the *Amphion* at Cortelazzo in August 1809. Collingwood's midshipman, George Castle, is mentioned in the dispatch.

Two of the guns of Royal Sovereign stand guard below the Collingwood monument at Tynemouth

As a 15 year old midshipman George Castle fought at the Battle of Trafalgar from behind guns such as these and wrote a graphic account of his experience in a letter to his sister.

[Author's collection]

The Collingwood Memorial in St Nicholas Cathedral, Newcastle

Erected in 1821, the memorial's inscription summarises the events of Collingwood's illustrious naval career. Every year, on Trafalgar Day, a wreath is still laid in his honour.

[Author's collection]

I hope and trust *Royal Oak* and *Alfred* are the only ones that will not be able to do their duty to good effect whenever you can bring the enemy to a second engagement and I think the *Alfred*, if not the *Royal Oak*, will be in tolerable order tomorrow.[9]

Hood's assessment proved to be correct and both ships took their place in the rear of the British line at the Battle of the Saintes on 12 April 1782. During the afternoon of a day-long encounter *Royal Oak* came up with the French *Glorieux* [74], by then a dismasted hulk lying motionless in a flat calm sea '...her decks heaped with dead and dying...a silent witness to the murderous efficiency of British gunnery'.[10] In what can only be described as an astonishing coincidence although Landless may not have been aware of it at the time, his old ship *Richmond*, now part of the French fleet, abandoned an attempt to tow *Glorieux* away from the battle as *Royal Oak* approached.[11] Later, towards the end of the action, *Ville de Paris* [104], flagship of the Comte de Grasse, struck her colours to *Barfleur*, Hood's flagship.

Ville de Paris was one of only four prizes taken by Rodney's fleet at the battle, a disappointing count given the decisive nature of the British victory. It drew subsequent criticism from Hood who believed that three times that number might have been secured had Rodney ordered a more vigorous pursuit. As if to rub salt into the wound, only one of Rodney's prizes ever reached England. *Ville de Paris* and *Glorieux* both foundered in a hurricane in mid-Atlantic and *Hector* was so totally disabled that she had to be abandoned. The British *Ramillies* [74] and *Centaur* were also lost in the same storm. *Royal Oak* remained in the West Indies until the following year when, on his return to England, Landless renewed his association with Captain Hudson who had been given command of *Venus* [36]. He spent the following three years in her as a master's mate patrolling in home waters and eventually passed for lieutenant on 5 June 1786. Unfortunately, *Venus* paid off at Deptford later the same month and Landless was left without a ship and, in the context of peacetime, little immediate prospect of a commission to one. His response to unemployment came to have a significant impact on the rest of his naval career; Landless joined the East India Company.

His decision to do so was neither unusual nor surprising. The East India Company traditionally attracted naval officers to its marine service because their background and nautical knowledge was well suited to handling large, well armed and comprehensively manned East Indiamen. Captain Timmins of *Royal George* had also been a naval lieutenant when he joined the Company and fourth mate of *Halsewell* in 1786, of the same age and experience as Landless, had recently been lieutenant of *Scipio* [64].[12] It seems likely that Landless, once again, benefited from 'connexions' in his application to join the East India Company; Admiral Roddam's brother, Collingwood Roddam, and a relative of his mentor, Lieutenant Younghusband, who was chief mate of *Middlesex*.

Thetis, the vessel Landless joined as sixth mate in October 1786, was a new ship of 804 tons built by Randall at Blackwall and only recently launched. His pay was a mere £2-5-0 per month, less than his half-pay as a naval lieutenant, but it was guaranteed for the duration of the voyage and might easily be supplemented by the proceeds of private trade, one of the perks of an officer in the East India Company.

In October 1786 *Thetis* was hauled from Randall's dock at Blackwall and moored in the Long Reach where she began to provision for her maiden voyage to Bengal. Justinian Nutt, captain of *Thetis*, was an experienced commander who joined the Company in 1762 and had served both as mate and captain of *Duke of Kingston* between 1772 and 1783.[13] On Boxing Day 1786 *Thetis* slipped down river to Gravesend to embark her guns, passengers and 183 soldiers of the 73rd Regiment of Foot. By New Years Day 1787 she was anchored in the Downs awaiting a favourable wind. The passage out to Bengal was generally uneventful and took four months to complete. Several members of the 73rd Regiment died during the voyage and one of the mates was washed overboard and drowned, '…he unfortunately could not swim', according to a laconic reference in the logbook. A year after her departure from England, in January 1788, *Thetis* sailed from Calcutta laden with spices and Indian fabrics. On 8 March, off the Cape of Good Hope, *Thetis*:

> …shipt [sic] a sea over the poop quarter and main deck. The quantity of water on the different decks laid the ship down for some time before she recovered and a deal of water went down the different hatchways which makes us apprehend some of the cargo got damaged.[14]

After calling at St. Helena to embark passengers in April, *Thetis* arrived back in the Downs in June 1788. Landless mustered as fourth mate for his second voyage later the same year, this time to Bombay and China. He returned briefly to the Royal Navy between May and November 1790 when he mustered as a master's mate of *Royal William* [80], flagship of Admiral Roddam at Portsmouth, during the war scare surrounding the Nootka Sound Dispute. The crisis with Spain, however, was resolved diplomatically and Landless returned to Belford where he spent the following 18 months. In April 1792 he sailed as third mate of *Thetis* for a voyage to China direct although her departure was delayed by the Navy at Portsmouth when 43 seamen were pressed at Spithead.[15] Such a large number represented almost half of the seamen in the crew and it must have provoked loud protests from the East India Company, not only because it was unusual to press so many from the crew of an outward bound East Indiaman, but also because she was carrying several high-ranking passengers. Amongst them were three members of the Secret Superintending Committee and their servants bound to Canton as part of an East India Company initiative to establish an embassy there under Lord McCartney.[16]

In addition to her passengers, *Thetis* carried a mixed cargo of bale goods, food and drink and over 9,000 ingots of tin, arriving at Whampoa, the European anchorage below Canton, in September 1792. She returned to England with a cargo of tea, raw silk and nankeen in June 1793. Landless then returned to Northumberland where he married Mary Pinkerton, whose father was a tenant farmer at Belford. They set up home in Berwick before William returned to *Thetis* the following year as chief mate to a new captain. Henry Bullock was only three years older than Landless but had sailed 11 voyages to India and the Far East, two of them as first mate of *Thetis*. He was, therefore, already known to Landless and presumably there was a good deal of mutual respect between them. Bullock continued to command the ship until 1802. The voyage of 1794-95, to Bengal and Madras, was undertaken in wartime conditions and began at Plymouth in June 1794. *Thetis,* in company with three other East Indiamen and 70 sail of merchantmen bound south, formed part of a convoy escorted by 11 warships. For Landless it proved to be his final voyage to the sub-continent.

Having risen to become a chief mate his decision to leave the East India Company seems puzzling. One more voyage would probably have qualified him for a command and the access that would have given him to a substantial income through private trade. Bullock's appointment as captain of *Thetis* and his relative youth may have had some influence on his decision. Even with the experience of further voyages to India Landless needed a substantial sum of money, as much as £5,000, to purchase a command of his own since:

> An India command was by this time a piece of property which its owner could sell or pass on to a friend or relative on his retirement and which became part of his estate if he died in service.[17]

Another factor in his decision may have been related to his personal circumstances. On his return to England in November 1795 Landless discovered that his wife had died six months earlier leaving their infant son in the care of relatives. Since long and regular absences from home were the norm for commanders of East Indiamen he may have felt this was no longer practical. Besides, a return to the Royal Navy as a commissioned officer, in wartime, offered good opportunities for promotion and prize money. The major disadvantage lay principally in the loss of ten years seniority as a lieutenant. Landless was originally commissioned on 5 June 1786 but his subsequent service with the East India Company interrupted the continuity of his naval career. After a few months as an acting lieutenant of *Venerable*, Admiral Duncan's flagship, his status as a lieutenant was re-confirmed from 3 June 1796 and this became the date from which his seniority was taken.[18] The practical result was that he was placed at the bottom of the lieutenant's list despite his age and experience. By 1796 Landless was already in his mid-thirties and his prospects of promotion compared to younger men would certainly have compromised the remainder of his naval career had it not been for the continued patronage of Admiral Roddam and the subsequent support he received from Collingwood.

On the confirmation of his rank Landless was commissioned to *Glenmore* [36] a new frigate built at Woolwich and launched earlier that year. *Glenmore* has been described as '…perhaps the most Scottish ship ever in the Royal Navy'.[19] She was built from fir timber felled in the Great Glen and almost all of her officers were Scottish including George Duff, captain of *Glenmore*, who was well connected in the Scottish aristocracy. Duff was later killed at Trafalgar when captain of *Mars*. Landless remained with *Glenmore* for a year patrolling in home waters and was then commissioned to *Inflexible* at The Nore. It proved to be a short but difficult appointment in the aftermath of the Great Mutinies of 1797.

Inflexible was acknowledged to have been 'the incendiary ship' of the mutiny at The Nore. Her seamen were the first to send unpopular officers ashore and amongst the last to return to their duty. Within a week of Landless' arrival on board Richard Parker, self-acknowledged leader of the mutiny, was brought before a court martial already a condemned man. He was respectful and suitably contrite in accepting his sentence but expressed his hope that '…my life will be the only sacrifice…I trust it will be thought a sufficient atonement'.[20]

Parker was hanged from the yardarm of *Sandwich* [98] at Sheerness in full view of the Fleet on 30 June 1797. His plea for clemency for other mutineers was largely acknowledged. Most of the 400 seamen brought before courts martial were subsequently pardoned, although 59 received death sentences of whom 29 were actually executed. All of the seamen of *Inflexible* were pardoned largely because the ringleaders escaped. When it became obvious that the mutiny had collapsed, three boats put off from the ship and rowed around to Faversham where 20 seamen 'requisitioned' a small sloop, *Good Intent,* sailed it to France and surrendered themselves to the French authorities at Calais. What became of them after that is a story yet to be told.[21]

In fulfilling his lieutenant's commission to join *Inflexible* William Landless, once again, witnessed the aftermath of one of the notable naval events of that era. He left *Inflexible* in September 1797 to spend the following four years as a lieutenant of two former Dutch warships, *Zealand* [64] and *Overyssel* [64], on the North Sea station. Both vessels were successive flagships of Vice-Admiral Skeffington Lutwidge, a benign and amiable character, who was a friend and confident of Horatio Nelson. Lutwidge had been second in command to Constantine Phipps during the expedition to the Arctic in search of a North West passage in 1773 and, as captain of *Carcass* [8], had agreed to take Nelson, then aged 15, as a midshipman. Lutwidge was later the source of the story about Nelson and the polar bear and the latter, by that time a Vice-Admiral himself, visited *Overyssel* en route to the Baltic and the Battle of Copenhagen in 1801. It seems likely that Landless met and dined with Nelson on that occasion. By comparison with some of his earlier experiences these were generally uneventful years and successive commissions to ships stationed in home waters allowed Landless to keep in regular touch with his family.

In August 1800 his young son, William, died at Berwick aged six and a developing crisis in his father's affairs stimulated some surviving correspondence with Thomas Adams, an Alnwick solicitor. George Landless, William's father, had fallen into arrears of rent for his farm at Belford Mill, a modest smallholding consisting of, 'five cart horses, one galloway, four young horses, two cows, five young beasts and a sow, with all the corn in the yard and the husbandry utensils.'[22]

The estate evicted George Landless from his farm in December 1800 and soon after Lieutenant Landless stepped in to protect what remained of his father's interests. He wrote to Adams from the *Overyssel* in September 1801:

> I trust your goodness will pardon the liberty I am taking in addressing you on the subject of my father's effects but as you are well acquainted with the situation of his affairs and apprehend have in your possession all of the writings respecting his houses in Belford which I have some reason to believe he is entitled to make over to me should he apply to you for that purpose hope you will procure the proprietor of the Belford estate's consent if necessary... will esteem it a favour if you will employ any person you think proper to let him draw up a Deed of Gift making the houses totally over to me without any kind of exception or proviso whatever...as I cannot think of doing anything for my father until everything is secured in the strongest manner

to prevent them from going into people's hands that have no right to them and have it not in their power to afford him the smallest assistance.[23]

Adams advised Landless that he would need a licence from the proprietor of the Belford estate, Hon. A.G. Onslow, before he could act on his behalf. Accordingly, Landless addressed a letter to Onslow in which he outlined the circumstances that had obliged his father to quit his tenancy at Belford Mill '…from old age and infirmity'. He explained that his father:

> …had nothing to live on but what he depends on me for in consequence of which I mean to allow him a yearly salary and he wishes to make over to me the three houses he has in Belford on a lease of three lives which he built in Mr. Dixon's time and as I am the eldest son hope it will make no difference to you my being put in possession of them during my father's life which will materially serve both him and me.

Landless left *Overyssel* in October 1801 but was clearly anxious to settle his father's affairs before accepting a new commission from the Admiralty for '…being an officer in H.M. Navy makes my stay in the country very uncertain from the present appearance of things'.[24]

Unfortunately none of the subsequent correspondence seems to have survived but his letters suggest that he enjoyed a comfortable income, sufficient for him to provide his father with an annuity, which would certainly have proved difficult on a lieutenant's salary of £72 a year. Moreover, his time in the service of the East India Company and his share of prize money enabled him to invest in local business. His letter to Onslow, for example, was addressed care of Messrs. Johnson and Todd; the latter was a proprietor of the Berwick Ropery, established in 1794, and a shareholder in the Old Shipping Company. It may not have been simple coincidence that the names of both Richard and Joseph Todd appeared regularly in the annual accounts between 1802 and 1808 above those of Elizabeth, James and George Landless.[25]

Despite his anxiety that he might be called away before he was able to settle his father's affairs, the Peace of Amiens in 1802 enabled Landless to remain in Northumberland for almost two years. He seems to have acquired some property at Belford and an interest in the farm at Easington although he does not appear to have purchased it at this stage. Soon after the resumption of the war against Napoleon, in August 1803, Landless was commissioned to Collingwood's flagship *Venerable* for the second time in his career. *Venerable* was neither an old nor unseaworthy warship but the punishing conditions of regular blockade duties off Brest and in the Bay of Biscay exposed structural weaknesses which threatened the integrity of the ship and the lives of the crew:

> I came in from the sea with orders from the Admiralty to refresh the ship's company and, poor creatures, they have almost been worked to death ever since. We began by discovering slight defects in the ship and the farther we went into the examination the more important they appeared until at last she was discovered to be so completely rotten as to be unfit for sea. We have been sailing for the last six months with only a sheet of copper between us and eternity![26]

Lieutenant Landless was able to spend a brief spell at Belford during the summer of 1804 as *Venerable* was refitting before joining Collingwood on *Dreadnought* in August 1804. When he returned to Northumberland three years later he had been promoted Commander. Such rapid promotion seemed unlikely in October 1805.

A week before Trafalgar Landless, not for first time, made a poor choice at a critical stage in his naval career. He declined Collingwood's invitation to move with him from *Dreadnought*, in which he was third lieutenant, to become second lieutenant of *Royal Sovereign*. Collingwood was clearly puzzled and seemed irritated by his refusal. He subsequently explained:

> When Lord Nelson came out and I was to go in the *Royal Sovereign* he thought all promotion was at an end and pretending a complaint in his eyes declined going with me that he might return to England in the *Dreadnought*. I gave him good time to consider it and at last he determined to go home. I hope Admiral Roddam will see that it is entirely Landless's own affair.[27]

His decision was probably influenced by personal rather than professional reasons. *Dreadnought* was foul with weed and desperately in need of a refit. She was under orders to sail to England flying the flag of Sir Robert Calder who was returning to face a court martial for his conduct in an action against Villeneuve's fleet off Cape Finisterre earlier that year. As it turned out Nelson allowed Calder to return to England in his own flagship, *Prince of Wales* [90], so that Landless and *Dreadnought* remained with Nelson's fleet off Cadiz and subsequently fought at Trafalgar. His experience of the battle was, therefore, considerably different to that endured by the officers and crew of *Royal Sovereign*. Whereas Collingwood's flagship famously opened the action with the combined fleet at noon, *Dreadnought* was ordered to keep out of the way of faster ships and did not join the battle until 1:30 p.m. Once she did so, however, her much vaunted gunnery proved decisive in forcing several Spanish ships, already damaged by the earlier fighting, to withdraw or strike their colours. *San Juan Nepomunceno* [74] surrendered to *Dreadnought* about 2:30 p.m. and Captain Conn sent a prize crew on board before sailing in pursuit of *Principe de Asturias* [112], flagship of Admiral Gravina.

At 4:00 p.m. Collingwood signalled for *Dreadnought* to call off the pursuit and join other relatively undamaged ships to prevent an attempt by the French Admiral Dumanoir to recover some of the prizes. *Dreadnought*'s casualties at Trafalgar amounted to seven killed and 26 wounded, more than many other ships in the British fleet, but less than a quarter of those suffered by the crew of *Royal Sovereign*.

Landless continued in *Dreadnought* under Captain John Conn and Rear-Admiral, the Earl of Northesk, until December 1805 when Collingwood, aware of Admiral Roddam's desire to have him promoted, gave him command of an armed merchant ship, *Lord Eldon* [14], which he described as '…a bad vacancy that nothing can be expected from', but in the circumstances he considered it expedient '…merely to keep him here until something good happens'.[28] He then wrote several agitated letters to Lord Barham from *Queen* [98] in March/April 1806 'on the subject of appointments' expressing his disappointment that:

> The only officer for whom I was particularly anxious or whom I recommended to your Lordship to be promoted has been passed over unnoticed…Lieutenant Landless is an old and valuable officer. He has followed me from ship to ship the whole war and I did hope that my earnest recommendation to your Lordship might have gained him favour. I cannot help thinking that there must have been something in my conduct of which your Lordship did not approve and that you have marked your disapprobation by this denying to my dependants and friends what was given so liberally to other ships in the fleet.[29]

It was probably a change of ministry in England rather than Collingwood's indignation that eventually worked in his favour. By the time Collingwood's letters reached the Admiralty, Barham had been replaced as First Lord by Charles Grey, Lord Howick, a fellow Northumbrian who used his influence to satisfy Collingwood's request. Landless was promoted commander in August 1806 and commissioned to *Morgiana* [16], sloop of war.

Morgiana had a complement of 62 men and was armed with fourteen 18-pounder and two 6-pounder guns. She had formerly been a French privateer captured by a British frigate in the Bay of Biscay in 1800. She sailed regularly from Gibraltar operating against French and Spanish commerce. In September 1806 Landless stopped and searched an enemy merchant ship and sent Thomas Dawson, a 26-year-old midshipman from Morpeth, and several seamen on board as a prize crew.[30] Then in December while cruising off Cape St. Mary at the western edge of the Gulf of Cadiz, *Morgiana* sighted 'a strange sail' and set off in pursuit of it. The logbook entry continued:

> Thursday 4 December 1806
>
> At noon a light breeze made all sail possible in chase of the strange sail. At 3:15 out cutter and at 5:30 the cutter boarded the chase and at 6:00 came up with her. The chase proved to be a Spanish settee from Vera Cruz bound to Cadiz. At 7:00 made sail with prize in company. Cape St. Mary ENE, 32 miles.[31]

Landless took 21 Spanish seamen as prisoners at two-thirds allowance and put his own prize crew on board the settee. Both ships moored at Gibraltar on 12 December where Landless discovered the true value of his capture. Collingwood received the news of his former lieutenant's success just over a week later and wrote:

> Landless has taken an exceedingly good prize, a boat from La Vera Cruz, very small but laden with cochineal, indigo etc. which will give him more prize money than I have got since I came out, except for Trafalgar.[32]

The prize's name *La Nueva Paloma* was an alias. Her real name was *Santo Christo del Grao* and her capture was registered and adjudicated by the Deputy Registrar of the Vice-Admiralty Court at Gibraltar on 25 December 1806. The vessel and her cargo were condemned for sale five days later. Unfortunately, there appears to be no surviving record of the amount of prize money Landless eventually received but it must have been substantial, possibly as much as £5,000, remitted to him by the prize agents Messrs. Archbold and Johnson.[33] *Morgiana* resumed her patrols off the Spanish coast until May 1807 when Landless was ordered to escort a convoy back to England arriving safely at Portsmouth in July. *Morgiana* was then paid off at Chatham on 13 August 1807 and Landless returned to his home in Belford after an absence of more than three years.

He seems to have purchased the farm at Easington sometime during the following year, probably with the prize money he had won since Trafalgar.[34] He was certainly living there when he married for a second time in Edinburgh in July 1808, although he continued to solicit the Admiralty for a new commission. In December 1807 he received a letter from Admiral Lord Gambier promising to pass on a letter of support from Collingwood to Lord Mulgrave, First Lord of the Admiralty, and Collingwood continued to write from *Ocean* on his behalf throughout the following year. In July 1808, for example, a few days before his marriage, Collingwood wrote confidently to Landless 'I shall be very glad to hear that you succeed in getting employment',[35] and later the same year in a letter to his sister, commented rather sarcastically 'I hear that Landless has got a ship and so he will get clear of his wife as soon as he did of the other, in a different way'.[36] It was a cruel joke. Collingwood was clearly aware that Landless had recently re-married and, despite his prediction, Landless chose not to tempt fate a second time.

On 29 August 1808 Landless was appointed to *Redpole* [16],

a new sloop recently launched and fitting out at Portsmouth, but he declined the appointment writing back to Sir John Barrow at the Admiralty on 3 September:

> I acknowledge receipt of your letter of the 29th ultimo informing me of my Lords Commissioners of the Admiralty having been pleased to appoint me to the command of H.M. sloop *Redpole* at Portsmouth and I regret extremely that I am under the painful necessity of requesting you to state to their Lordships that I have been for some time past very unwell with a severe fit of the gout which has rendered me unfit for an active situation at present but when I get well I will be most happy to accept any employment their Lordships may be pleased to honour me with.[37]

Landless probably knew that the chances of receiving another seagoing commission were remote. Whether his illness was genuine or simply an excuse to spend time with his new wife, his decision to refuse the appointment to *Redpole* effectively ended his naval career. He was 46 years old, his patron Admiral Roddam died earlier the same year and Collingwood, in declining health, was unlikely to renew his support when there were so many other younger and perhaps more deserving officers in search of a command. Moreover, since the proportion of commanders in the Royal Navy rose much faster than captains or lieutenants during the Napoleonic War, there was an insufficient number of vessels available for them to command. In 1812, for example, there were 586 commanders on the Navy List but only 168 sloops and gun brigs available for them to command.[38] In refusing *Redpole*, Landless became what the naval historian Nicholas Rodger has described as '…the typical commander of the Napoleonic War; a middle-aged officer with no further prospects'.[39]

Instead, he became a gentleman farmer and devoted himself to the consolidation and improvement of his estate at Easington, no doubt encouraged by the reputation and techniques of the celebrated George Culley, who had purchased the neighbouring Easington Grange estate with his brother Matthew in 1801.[40] Landless built a new farmhouse and outbuildings, improved the cottages and garths for his workers and encouraged the adoption of turnip cultivation as part of a system of crop rotation. Like the Culleys he appointed a steward, Adam Thompson, to manage the farm, enclosed the fields with thorn hedges and built a water mill to thresh as well as grind his corn.[41] In the decade after Waterloo, William Landless established himself as a socially active and highly respected member of the Belford community. He was a member of the Select Vestry after 1820 and of the committee appointed to oversee the re-building of Belford Parish Church in 1825 although he did not live to see it completed. William Landless died at Easington on 2 January 1826 aged 63; his second wife Margaret died only a few months later. He was buried at Ford beside his son and his first wife. The estate at Easington, '...313 acres of very superior land producing great crops of turnips and every kind of grain and commanding an extensive sea prospect', was advertised for sale by his executors at The Blue Bell Inn on 23 May 1826.[42] Following the death of his second wife, his nephews and nieces became the principal beneficiaries of his will.[43]

References

1. Hughes, E., *The Private Correspondence of Admiral Lord Collingwood*, Navy Records Society (NRS) (1957), Collingwood to his sister, 31 October 1808.

2. Belford Local History Society (BLHS). Biannual rental rolls of Belford Estate 1766-1799. I am grateful to David Morrison for this information.

3. http://genform.genealogy.com/landless [Accessed 30 June 2008].

4.   Berwick-upon-Tweed Record Office (BRO), Old Shipping Company Valuations and Dividend Payments, BRO 10/2/1.

5.   *Terrible* [74] was so badly damaged during the fighting on 5 September that she became unseaworthy. On 11 September she was abandoned and destroyed by fire.

6.   The National Archives (TNA), ADM 1/5319. Evidence presented at the Court Martial of Captain Charles Hudson.

7.   TNA, ADM 1/5319.

8.   Spinney, D., *Rodney*, Allen & Unwin (1969), p. 394.

9.   TNA, PRO 30/20/26/2. Rear-Admiral Samuel Hood to Admiral Rodney, 10 April 1782.

10.   Spinney, *Rodney*, p. 402.

11.   The incident is described in Hannay, D., *George Brydges Rodney (1719-1792)*, McMillan (1910), p. 208.

12.   Sutton, J., *Lords of the East*, Conway Maritime Press (2000), p. 78.

13.   Farrington, A.J., *A biographical index of the names of Maritime serving officers of the East India Company 1660-1834*, British Library (BL).

14.   BL, L/MAR/B/387A, Journal of the ship *Thetis* 1786-88.

15.   BL, L/MAR/B/387C, Journal of the ship *Thetis* 1792-93.

16.   Sutton, *Lords of the East*, p. 13.

17.   Sutton, p. 53.

18.   TNA, ADM 9/4/989.

19.   Lavery, B., *Nelson's Fleet at Trafalgar*, National Maritime Museum (NMM) (2004), pp. 74-75.

20.   Mainwaring, G.E. and Dobree, B., *The Floating Republic*, The Cresset Library, p. 240.

21.   Mainwaring and Dobree, *Floating Republic*, p. 236.

22.   BLHS, John Dinning to Thomas Adams, 20 October 1800.

23.   BLHS, Lt. William Landless to Thomas Adams, 11 September 1801.

24.   BLHS, Lt. William Landless to Hon. A.G. Onslow, 16 March 1802.

25.   BRO, 10/2/1. George Landless may well have been a younger brother.

26. Newnham Collingwood, G.L., *A Selection from the Public and Private Correspondence of Vice-Admiral Lord Collingwood*, James Ridgeway (1829). Collingwood to John Erasmus Blackett, 16 December 1803.

27. Hughes, *Correspondence of Admiral Lord Collingwood*, Collingwood to his brother, 3 April 1806.

28. Hughes, *Correspondence of Admiral Lord Collingwood*, Collingwood to his brother, 3 April 1806. *Lord Eldon* was a ship of 335 tons and 14 guns built and registered at Sunderland in 1801. She was transferred to Portsmouth in February 1805 and sailed for Gibraltar later the same year where she was employed as a convoy escort. See Tyne Wear Archives Service (TWAS), MF 1490, Sunderland Register of Ships (No.15, 1801) and *Newcastle Courant*, 21 December 1805.

29. Newnham Collingwood, *Public and Private Correspondence of Vice-Admiral Lord Collingwood*, Collingwood to Lord Barham, 28 March 1806.

30. TNA, ADM 36/17131. Muster Book of the *Morgiana*.

31. TNA, ADM 51/1637. Journal of the *Morgiana*. A Settee was a single-decked vessel with a sharp prow and carrying lateen sails. They were commonly used by traders in the Mediterranean, particularly around the coast of North Africa. See for example, Admiral Smyth, W.H., *The Sailors' Word Book*, (1867). A contemporary description defined them as 'A ship with two masts equipped with triangular sails, commonly called lateen. These vessels are peculiar to the Mediterranean and are generally navigated by Italians, Greeks and Mohammedans.' Cadell, T., *Universal Dictionary of the Marine or Falconer's Marine Dictionary*, (London) 1780.

32. Newnham Collingwood, *Public and Private Correspondence*, Collingwood to Lady Collingwood, 20 December 1806.

33. TNA, HCA 49/99 and ADM 7/356.

34. A.G. Onslow, nephew of Abraham Dixon, inherited the estate after the death of his uncle in 1783, but sold it to various speculators in 1805-06. William Landless appears to have purchased his farm at Easington from them at an estimated cost of between £7-10,000.

35. www.artfact.com [Accessed 07/02/2008]. Lyon & Turnbull, Edinburgh, 2006. Lot 313: British Navy, Collingwood, Lord Admiral and Admiral Gambier. Lot 313 was an item in an auction sale of antiquarian books viz: Davies, W., *A Fine Old English Gentleman, exemplified in the Life and Character of Lord Collingwood*, (1875). Pasted inside the front end cover

was an autographed note to Landless signed by Collingwood and dated 26 July 1808 together with an autographed letter from Admiral Lord Gambier promising to forward a letter from Lord Collingwood to Lord Mulgrave and dated December 1807.

36.   Newnham Collingwood, *Public and Private Correspondence*, Collingwood to his sister, 31 October 1808.

37.   TNA, ADM 1/2077. Landless to Admiralty, 3 September 1808.

38.   Lavery, B., *Nelson's Navy: The Ships, Men and Organisation 1793-1815*, Part IV, p. 98.

39.   Rodger, N.A.M. Commissioned officers' careers in the Royal Navy 1690-1815, *Journal of Maritime History*, (June 2001), pp. 1-22.

40.   Orde, A. The Culleys and Farm Management, *Northern History*, XLI, 2, (Sept. 2004), pp. 327-338.

41.   *Newcastle Courant*, 6 & 13 May 1826.

42.   *Newcastle Courant*, 6 & 13 May 1826.

43.   University of Durham, Dept. of Palaeography and Diplomatic, No. 40, 1820. Will of William Landless, 5 August 1820.

'Tell Thompson's father that his son behaved so admirably in the battle that if he had served his time I would have made him a lieutenant the same day. He is wounded in the arm but would not quit his duty upon the deck until at the very closing of the action his leg was broken by a large splinter.'

[Admiral Collingwood to his sister
25 October 1805]

Collingwood's Midshipmen

Granville Thompson 1788-1817
George Castle 1790-1826

All the naval officers who served at sea during the French Wars began their careers under the patronage of admirals and post-captains whose right to enter young gentlemen onto the muster books of the vessels they commanded reflected the status of their position and was rarely, if ever, challenged. Before 1815 the Admiralty exercised little control over the number of young men recruited by individual captains or the character of their social and educational background.[1] After 1794 the minimum age of entry for 'young gentlemen intended for the sea service' was set at 11 years for the sons of naval officers but 13 or 14 was usual for the majority. Midshipmen were allowed £6 a year until they qualified as a lieutenant and parents were expected to provide clothes and necessary equipment on entry. A family, political or professional connection was always the means by which young men began their naval career and it was often used to influence their subsequent advancement as well.

Collingwood had much to say about midshipmen:

> 'You may have heard that I am reckoned rather queer in the promotion of young men', he wrote to a correspondent in April 1809, 'I advance a great many who have not a friend to speak for them while those I respect most in the world sometimes plead in vain. Those who are diligent and promise to be useful officers never miscarry'.[2]

Alternately, those who lacked competence or motivation tried his patience and provoked his censure:

> 'I had three Richardsons here the other day,' he wrote to his father-in-law from *Excellent* in July 1795, 'but shall carry only one to sea…the eldest was not a person by any means entitled and if I had known what state he was in before he came here I would not have received such an expense and burden on the service'.[3]

Granville Thompson and George Castle clearly possessed the qualities Collingwood considered necessary to a successful officer. Thompson was the son of a Newcastle merchant whose premises in Side were close to where Collingwood himself was born. He was 15 years old when Collingwood agreed to take him on *Venerable* in 1803. George Castle was 13. His father, Samuel, was a Durham solicitor and business associate of Erasmus Blackett who recommended the boys to Collingwood. They travelled to Portsmouth in August 1803 where they mustered to the receiving ship *Le Puissant* [74] for onward passage to *Venerable* which was patrolling with the Channel Fleet off Ushant. Castle's father recorded the process of initiation:

> Expecting my wife home today…thank God I am able to say she arrived safe in the mail this morning after performing the journey and managing the business very satisfactorily. She saw my son on board the *Puissant* receiving ship last Monday to go from thence in the *Magnificent*, Captain Jarvis, to Admiral Collingwood in the Channel Fleet. He was in great spirits and after they had relieved themselves by a few tears in private the lad in a most manly way requested his mother not to go to the waterside with him for he did not wish either to heighten her distress or his own or be seen whimpering. She saw him however out of the high room of an inn…thus is launched into the busy world (I have the comfort to hope), another hero for further glory in future for his country and heaven will bless the kind exertions you have bestowed on him.[4]

On 27 September Collingwood wrote to Castle's parents confirming the safe arrival of their son, 'in good health and spirits', and added encouragingly, ' He seems a sprightly, spirited youth and there is no doubt will in due time make a good officer'.[5]

A subsequent letter from Collingwood written on 10 October indicates that 'the two youngsters' had been shipped to the Admiral with a number of 'Newcastle volunteers' and another, more experienced midshipman, James Graydon from East Rainton near Durham, who was returning from leave.[6]

The boys followed Collingwood from ship to ship throughout 1804-05 eventually moving with him from *Dreadnought* to *Royal Sovereign* ten days before Trafalgar. Each of them survived the battle although Thompson and Graydon were both wounded.

George Castle was unscathed and wrote an eye witness account of the battle in a letter to his sister written from Gibraltar on 3 November 1805. Notwithstanding some exaggeration and inaccuracy, Castle's detailed account of the battle offers a fascinating glimpse of the Trafalgar experience from the perspective of a 15-year-old boy. He was stationed at one of the 32 pounders on the lower gun deck and recalled *Royal Sovereign's* duel with *Santa Ana*:

> A great three-decker…so close that it was impossible to miss her…I looked once out of our stern ports but I saw nothing but French and Spaniards round firing at us in every direction…we had seven ships on us at once – the *Belleisle* was next to us in the action…likewise the *Tonnant*. We began the engagement at a quarter past twelve and did not cease firing until three.[7]

Granville Thompson's experience of Trafalgar was clearly more traumatic principally because he fought from a more dangerous and exposed position on the upper gun deck. In an early account of the battle the *Newcastle Courant* reported how Thompson:

> …is said to have exhibited astonishing feats of personal intrepidity. Though severely wounded in the arm he refused to go below persevering with his situation upon the deck until a splinter broke his leg and compelled him to be carried to the surgeon.[8]

As Castle wrote an account of the battle to his sister, Thompson, with the rest of the wounded, was carried to Gibraltar Hospital where he spent several months recovering from his injuries. He subsequently rejoined Collingwood on *Ocean* who promoted him master's mate and had him transferred to *Scout* [18], Commander William Raitt, on 5 July 1806. *Scout* was a sloop of war with a complement of 121 men, employed on convoy protection duties and offensive operations to disrupt French and Spanish trade. She was a relatively new ship built at Hull in 1804 and was amongst the first British ships to arrive at the scene of the Trafalgar battle the day after the action. On 23 October, in company with *Leviathan* [74], Collingwood ordered *Scout* to keep a close watch on the movements of the undamaged ships of the Combined Fleet at Cadiz. The following day she was involved in the evacuation of crews from the prizes after Collingwood ordered their destruction.[9]

Thompson's promotion to *Scout* came in the aftermath of a considerable turnover of former officers. During April 1806 her captain, Mackay, was superseded and two of his lieutenants, Jonathan Haskell and Thomas Allen, faced a court martial and were dismissed the Service a few weeks later. William Raitt, Mackay's replacement, was clearly an active and brave commander and Thompson saw plenty of action during the three years he served on the ship. Periodic references to him in Collingwood's correspondence indicate how the Admiral continued to take an interest in his progress.

Operating from Gibraltar, *Scout* regularly stopped and searched merchant ships of all nationalities suspected of smuggling or carrying illicit cargoes intended for enemy states. Many of them were American ships trading legitimately into the Mediterranean and the actions of *Scout* and her consort *Grasshopper* [18] must have caused some irritation and perhaps even diplomatic displeasure in Washington. For example, during three days between 9 and 11 July 1807, *Scout* stopped and boarded seven trading vessels, five of them American. On 20 July she recaptured an American brig off Europa Point taken earlier by a Spanish privateer.[10] The monotony of these stop and search patrols was occasionally punctuated by brisk engagements with privateers, gunboats and even Spanish troops firing from the shore. When off Cape Trafalgar on 14 July, attempting to capture a Spanish merchant ship close inshore, *Scout* and *Grasshopper* sent several boats to secure the vessel but:

...as the boats approached the beach we observed a number of soldiers in the bushes who opened a smart fire of musketry on the boats. At 3 p.m. the boats returned with James Williams, seaman, killed by the fire of the enemy. At 4 p.m. stood inshore and opened my fire of grape and case shot at the enemy in the bushes.[11]

Williams was buried at sea later the same day and both ships returned to Gibraltar a week later. During August they engaged Spanish gunboats protecting a large convoy bound into the Atlantic from Algeciras and later captured a Spanish schooner laden with cocoa and indigo, put a prize crew on board and carried it into Gibraltar. On 2 November, again in company with *Grasshopper*, they intercepted and engaged a convoy bound from Cadiz under escort of 12 Spanish gunboats. On this occasion the Yeoman of the Powder Room, Thomas Baxter, aged 29 from Whitby, was killed '...by a raking shot that came in at the larboard stern port'.[12] Thompson appears to have come through each of these encounters without injury but other members of the crew were wounded during various subsequent encounters recorded in Captain Raitt's logbook.

Thompson's former companion, George Castle, remained with Collingwood as a midshipman, first on *Queen* and then *Ocean*, until May 1808 when Collingwood sent him into the frigate *Amphion* [32], Captain William Hoste, a protégé of Nelson and one of the best young captains in the Navy. Collingwood thought highly of his abilities as a frigate captain and ordered him to cruise in the Adriatic where there were good prospects of prize money. After Napoleon defeated the Austrian army at the battle of Wagram in 1809, French troops dominated both shores of the Adriatic and their coastal garrisons relied almost exclusively on maritime trade for their supplies. Most of it was carried in trabaccolos, small, two-masted vessels carrying lugsails and crewed by six or seven men. They were no match for a well-armed frigate like *Amphion* and usually surrendered without resistance. During the last quarter of 1808 Hoste captured 38 merchant ships and sent 32 of them as prizes to Malta, including one whose cargo, according to her part-owner, was worth £20,000.[13]

In November 1808, when *Amphion* was cruising off Trieste, Castle witnessed the successful conclusion of one of the epic escape stories of the Napoleonic War. Lieutenants Maurice Hewson and Donat Henchy O'Brien together with a ship's surgeon, Archibald Barklimore, had escaped from the fortress of Bitche '...the Colditz of the Napoleonic War' where they had been incarcerated after several earlier but unsuccessful attempts to escape. On 15 September 1808, using rope made from linen sheets, they descended more than 200 feet from the ramparts of the castle and made their way across southern Germany to Austria, at that time still in an uneasy alliance with France, and eventually to Trieste on the Adriatic where they were delighted to discover that *Amphion* was cruising off the coast. On the evening of 7 November, with the help of the British Vice-Consul, they hired a boat and sailed in search of the frigate:

> Before day we weighed our grapnel, and were about to proceed...when we observed a boat pulling towards us which proved to be one from the *Amphion*, commanded by Captain Hoste. At first we concealed ourselves imagining that it might have been a Russian Man-of-War boat sent after us – how great then was our joy to find ourselves under a British flag.[14]

It is conceivable that Castle was in the boat that rescued them, since by that time he was an experienced midshipman familiar with the organisation and management of boat work.

For much of 1809 Hoste was the senior officer commanding British naval forces in the Adriatic and under his command Castle was involved in a number of sharp engagements, amphibious operations and boat attacks. The most notable was the cutting out and capture of six Franco-Italian gunboats together with seven merchant trabaccolos at Cortelazzo, a small port between Venice and Trieste, in August 1809. Captain Hoste's account of the action was subsequently published in the *London Gazette* and Castle's name, together with those of other officers and midshipmen involved in the attack, was included in his dispatch.[15] During the period in which Castle served in *Amphion*, Hoste captured or destroyed over 200 merchant ships, attacked shipping in ports throughout the northern Adriatic and established a base of operations on the island of Lissa. When he left Captain Hoste and returned to Collingwood's flagship, *Ville de Paris*, at Mahon on 21 February 1810, no doubt expecting to return to England with the Admiral, Castle was entitled to a midshipman's share of several thousand pounds in prize money.[16] But his anticipation of this windfall was tempered by the death of Admiral Collingwood two weeks later, and he must have feared for his prospects of promotion now that his patron was dead.

While Castle was serving in the Adriatic, Thompson found himself in several encounters off the French coast, between Marseilles and the Rhone, in June and July 1809. He commanded one of *Scout's* boats in cutting-out seven French merchant ships from a small harbour east of Cape Croisette on 14 June, and was in action again the following month. The gallantry he displayed in each of these engagements became another turning point of his career. Collingwood wrote to his sister from *Ville de Paris*

> …the ship young Thompson belongs to has had a severe action and he is wounded. He has a slug in his leg but is recovering. He will fight himself into a lieutenancy, I hope, very soon.[17]

On 28 July 1809 *Scout* had been patrolling near Marseilles when she was attacked by two French warships of 18 and 20 guns. The engagement lasted for over two hours during which time the largest of the French brigs attempted to board *Scout* by running her bowsprit into the starboard quarter of the British sloop but the attack was repulsed. Meanwhile, according to Captain Raitt's log:

> The other brig keeping up a heavy fire of round and grape shot within musket shot, both brigs being full of troops and at the same time receiving heavy fire of shot and shells from the batteries on shore. At 3:30 p.m. got clear of the largest having all of our starboard chain and running rigging cut to pieces...but at 4 p.m. observed seven sail of gunboats coming out of the harbour and standing towards us. Having rendered the largest brig a complete wreck but from the circumstances of our standing rigging being so much cut up, our sails cut to pieces, boom shot away and a number of killed and wounded I was under the necessity to haul off....[18]

With a tottering mast and damaged rigging they were lucky to evade capture. *Scout's* casualties were four killed and 31 wounded including Captain Raitt and Granville Thompson. William Houghton, one of the Royal Marines, died of his wounds several days later. They reached Gibraltar on 9 August where Thompson was admitted to the hospital for the second time in his short career. After his recovery Collingwood had him transferred to the flagship on 12 October 1809 and wrote from Port Mahon in November: 'I have made young Thompson a lieutenant and I hope he will deserve it.'[19]

It proved to be one of the last promotions he was able to make. Collingwood's health declined rapidly during the winter of 1809-10 and he spent much of his time ashore in the house he rented at

El Fonduco overlooking the harbour at Mahon. He could barely walk and ate very little as his stomach tumour grew. He resigned his commission as Commander-in-Chief Mediterranean Fleet in February 1810 and handed over his responsibilities to Rear-Admiral Sir George Martin on 3 March. He sailed for England on 5 March but died on board his flagship *Ville de Paris* two days later.[20] Fittingly, perhaps, his body was returned to England in a Tyne-built frigate, *Nereus* [32], launched from Simon Temple's yard at South Shields the year before. Collingwood's remains lay in state at Greenwich before he was buried in St. Paul's Cathedral next to Nelson in May 1810.

Thompson's first commission as a lieutenant was to the sloop *Kingfisher* [18], Captain Ewell Tritton, which he joined at Gibraltar on 2 December 1809. *Kingfisher* was a similar vessel to *Scout* and employed on similar duties, although after Spain joined the allies against Napoleon these were discharged over a wider area of the Mediterranean. *Kingfisher*'s muster book also indicates that Thompson had a few more Northumbrian mariners to command than was the case in his previous ship. Joseph Mills, one of the quartermasters, was from Hexham and there were able seamen from Newcastle, Bamburgh, Sunderland and Whitby amongst the crew.[21]

In July 1810, after Ralph Standish the first lieutenant was killed in action, Thompson assumed that role until another officer could be appointed. *Kingfisher* spent much of 1810-11 patrolling in the Aegean usually in company with larger warships like the frigates *Belle Poule* [38] and the appropriately named *Leonidas* [36]. Malta was often used as a base for these operations although frequent visits there appear to have provoked increased drunkenness and indiscipline amongst the crew. Soon after her arrival at Valetta in October 1811 two seamen, John Henderson and John Bonnet, received 12 lashes each for 'insolence and smuggling liquor on board' and a third, Thomas Jones, was punished with 24 strokes of the cat for 'repeated drunkeness'.[22] *Kingfisher* remained in dock in Malta for over a month and there were several further bouts of punishment before the ship eventually sailed for Lissa in the Adriatic. Thompson, however, was not on board. He had been transferred to *Trident* [64] soon after arriving in Malta.

George Castle was eventually promoted lieutenant on 20 August 1811 and commissioned to *Blake* [74], Captain Edward Codrington, an aristocratic commander later famous as the admiral whose ships destroyed a combined Turkish/ Egyptian fleet at the battle of Navarino in 1827. He had been captain of *Orion* [74] at Trafalgar and was well respected for his courage and tactical ability. Castle served as the junior lieutenant of *Blake* for two years, principally while the ship was employed in support of British and Spanish forces confronting Napoleon's army in the Peninsular. During a skirmish with French troops near Tarragona in January 1812, Lieutenant Castle was captured by a squadron of French dragoons while waiting on shore at Salou to deliver a quantity of powder to the allied army but later escaped after they were forced to retreat by Spanish infantry.[23] In September 1812 he took part in a successful boat attack launched from *Blake* and *Franchise* [36], supported by Spanish troops, against shipping in Tarragona harbour. Several small prizes were taken and, according to Codrington's report, due to:

> The voluntary and unanimous request of the officers and crews of the two ships that the whole of whatever benefit may arise from the sale of the prizes shall be given to the troops in admiration of the valour and discipline which they showed upon the occasion.[24]

The gesture may well have reflected a genuine respect for the courage of the Spanish troops involved in the attack but in reality it was a pragmatic decision. The captured vessels were of little value and hardly worth the trouble of manning with prize crews for adjudication by the Admiralty Prize Court at Gibraltar.

Following further service off the coast of Catalonia, *Blake* returned to England and paid off in June 1813. After a few months of unemployment, no doubt spent with his family in Durham, Castle was commissioned to *Warrior* [74], Captain Lord Torrington, and served aboard her in the North Sea until March 1814.

Thompson was commissioned to four separate ships during the same period. He appears to have served on *Trident* for less than a year, returning to England in 1812 for the first time since joining Collingwood as a young midshipman. It was probably at this time that his portrait, now in the collection of the Laing Art Gallery, was taken. Thompson then received a short but unusual commission to *Brave* [80], formerly the French *Formidable*, [25] which was employed as a prison ship at Plymouth. Thereafter, Lieutenant Thompson was commissioned to *Euryalus*, the frigate Admiral Collingwood had transferred into after Trafalgar. She spent much of 1812-13 providing support for Wellington's army in the Peninsular and patrolling with the British fleet off Toulon. Finally, in 1814, Granville Thompson was commissioned to the frigate *Nereide* [38], another former French ship captured off Mauritius in 1810, in which he served, principally in home waters, until she paid off at the end of the war. Thompson then returned to his native Newcastle where he appears to have spent almost three years as a lieutenant on half pay.

George Castle was in the West Indies when Thompson returned home. In March 1814 he had been appointed to *Espiegle* [18], sloop of war, Commander Charles Mitchell. According to an account in James, *Naval History of Great Britain*, George Castle was one of the naval officers directly involved in the abortive attack on Fort Bowyer in September 1814. The attack was directed by Captain the Honourable Henry William Percy, sixth son of the Duke of Northumberland, who commanded *Hermes* [20] and included another Northumbrian officer, Commander John Brand Umfreville of *Childers* [18]. While the British ships bombarded the fort a force of 60 Royal Marines and 120 native troops were landed to storm the battery. According to James, Lieutenant Castle was given command of a detachment of this force and ordered to secure the Pass of Bonsecours, 27 miles to the east, to prevent any American reinforcements reaching the fort. However, since *Espiegle* was not amongst the British sloops involved in the Fort Bowyer attack it suggests that James' account may be in error although in view of Castle's experience of amphibious operations, he may well have been seconded for operations ashore. As it turned out the British attack was firmly resisted. In a confined anchorage with strong tidal streams, *Hermes'* anchor cable parted, she drifted aground under the guns of Fort Bowyer and was badly damaged. With 25 killed and 24 wounded Percy was forced to abandon the frigate where she lay and the operation was a complete failure.[26]

During 1814-15 *Espiegle* spent most of her time on the Leeward Islands station cruising against American commerce and was successful in taking several prizes before the Treaty of Ghent ended the war with the United States in February 1815. Soon after, however, Napoleon escaped from Elba and hostilities with France were resumed during what is known as Napoleon's Hundred Days. *Espiegle* remained in the West Indies and subsequently formed part of the naval force sent to cover an attack on the French island of Guadeloupe. Castle's ship supported the initial landings of 850 troops of the Royal York Rangers at Ance St. Sauveur on 8 August. The French garrison finally surrendered on 10 August 1815, almost two months after Waterloo.[27] *Espiegle* returned to England in 1816 and paid off at Portsmouth. Lieutenant Castle saw no further service after that although his one time companion, Granville Thompson, did.

In March 1817 he was commissioned as first lieutenant of the frigate *Larne* [20], Captain Abraham Lowe, then fitting out for a voyage to the West Indies; Thompson joined the ship at Spithead. After an uneventful passage lasting a month *Larne* anchored in

Carlisle Bay, Barbados on 10 April and Port Royal, Jamaica the following week.[28] These were familiar anchorages to thousands of naval officers of that era and although it was Thompson's first voyage there he had, no doubt, heard about them from other officers. Roddam, Collingwood, Landless and Rotheram had all served in the Caribbean early in their careers and George Castle had recently returned from those waters despite its notorious reputation as an unhealthy and fever-ridden cruising ground where, 'for the men serving in the ships, disease was an invisible and pitiless killer which struck without distinction'.[29]

During the first three years of the French Wars, 1793-1796, the combined losses of British servicemen in the West Indies amounted to 35,000. Soldiers belonging to various regiments of foot used to garrison the islands, or undertake amphibious operations against French or Spanish possessions, suffered most but tropical diseases like malaria and yellow fever often decimated the crews of warships as well. Soon after her arrival in the West Indies in 1801, the crew of *Brunswick* was struck by yellow fever and 287 men were entered on the sick list in a matter of days, many of them subsequently died. As late as 1827, 12 years after Waterloo, every sixth member of a ship's company died of disease while serving on the West Indies station.[30]

When *Larne* sailed into the waters off Florida and the Bahamas in September 1817 sickness had already broken out amongst the crew. The first to die was a seaman, John Smith, on 22 September and on 28 September while anchored off Salt Kay near Nassau, Captain Lowe recorded: '…at 11:40 a.m. departed this life Lieutenant Granville Thompson…at 5 p.m. five boats left the ship with the corpse'.[31]

Thompson's death from fever was all too familiar and his passing merited only a brief, laconic reference in the logbook. The extent of sickness amongst the crew was revealed over the days that followed. On 29 September a tent was erected onshore and five midshipmen and 15 men were accommodated there the next day. It soon proved inadequate however, on 1 October the Governor at Nassau acceded to Captain Lowe's request to use the hospital at the Artillery Barracks. By then he had 28 men sick. When it seemed that some of them showed signs of recovery, Lowe embarked his invalids and sailed from Nassau on 14 October, arriving at Port Royal ten days later. George Jeffries died onboard the same day and 30 members of the crew were sent to hospital for treatment.[32]

It had been Thompson's first and only voyage to the West Indies and he may have suffered some ill health during the Atlantic passage since his will was drawn up and witnessed when *Larne* was still a day out from Barbados. Thompson's will was proved in London on 2 May 1818. His obituary, which appeared in the *Newcastle Courant* on 10 January 1818, commemorated his service with Collingwood at Trafalgar and concluded that he had:

> ...acquired by his bravery in service the esteem of his brother officers while his domestic qualities justly endeared him to his family and a respectable circle of friends in private life.[33]

The circumstances of George Castle's family and his post-naval career on a lieutenant's half-pay are not certainly known. He returned to Durham in 1816 to discover that both his father and surviving brother had died during his absence in the West Indies. Matthias, his youngest brother, had been a lieutenant in the 70th Regiment but was tragically drowned in Lake Ontario, 'by the upsetting of a canoe',[34] on his 17th birthday. George married Jane Hearn Cook, the daughter of a master mariner, at Tynemouth in 1817, and may have been employed in the coasting trade for a few years after that. Sometime during the early 1820s the couple moved to Derbyshire, probably in search of a remedy for

Lieutenant Castle's deteriorating health. He died there, 'from a lingering illness', in March 1826 at the age of 36. His widow outlived him by almost 40 years. She died in an asylum at Dinsdale, near Darlington, in 1865.[35]

Despite their experience and obvious gallantry, it is doubtful if Thompson or Castle would ever have reached the rank of post-captain, had they lived. In the much smaller navy of the 1820s patronage and political influence assumed even greater importance than it had during the French Wars. Well-connected officers usually obtained the limited commissions available and those like Thompson and Castle whose reputations depended upon their wartime experience were increasingly overlooked. Unemployed lieutenants, like George Castle, became a feature of the post-war era. Amongst the cohort of officers who became lieutenants between 1810 and 1814 fewer than 30 per cent ever became post-captains and those that did sometimes waited as long as 20 years for their promotion.[36] As late as the 1840s almost half of the post-captains on the Navy List had never served afloat in that rank.[37]

Excepting the careers of Admiral Roddam and Collingwood himself, both of whom came from an earlier generation of naval officers, Rotheram, Landless, Thompson and Castle seem to have been typical of naval officers who joined the Royal Navy after 1775. Rotheram, of course, was an enigma and Landless compromised his opportunities for promotion by his decision to enter the East India Company. Thompson was fortunate to receive a commission after 1815 and may have advanced further had he lived, but Castle's prospects of further promotion were slim.

After 1815 the Admiralty gradually extended its control over the recruitment and training of naval officers so that by the outbreak of the Crimean War in 1853 over 70 per cent of new entrants were nominated by the Admiralty.[38] Rapid technological change in the construction, propulsion and armament of warships ushered in the age of the ironclad and transformed the character of the Victorian navy as well as the professional skills of its officers. Nevertheless, despite these changes, younger sons of later generations of Northumberland families continued to pursue careers in the Royal Navy. Several members of the Grey, Blackett and Swinburne families became Victorian admirals, others fought at Jutland in 1916. During the Second World War another Northumbrian officer, 'Joe' Baker-Cresswell (1901-1997), was captain of the destroyer *H.M.S. Bulldog* when he captured the enigma coding machine from U-110 on 9 May 1941. He was later awarded the DSO and became aide-de-camp to King George VI. In retirement he farmed the family estate at Budle, near Bamburgh, close to where Collingwood's lieutenant, William Landless, had purchased a farm at Easington from the proceeds of his prize money almost 200 years before.[39]

References

1. There was however a limit to the number of midshipmen permitted to serve on ships of different rates. A First Rate was allowed 24; Third Rates, 20; Fifth & Sixth Rates, 6. See, Lavery, B., *Nelson's Navy*, Conway Maritime Press, (1989), Part IV, p. 92.

2. Hughes, E., *The Private Correspondence of Admiral Lord Collingwood*, Navy Records Society (NRS), (1957), Admiral Collingwood to Mrs. Stead, April 1809.

3. Northumberland Record Office (NRO), ZBL 247, Collingwood to J.E. Blackett, 8 July 1795.

4. NRO, ZBL 228, Samuel Castle to J.E. Blackett, 18 September 1803.

5. NRO, ZBL 228, Admiral Collingwood to Samuel Castle, 27 September 1803.

6. Newcastle Central Library, Letters from Captain Cuthbert Collingwood to Dr. Carlyle of Inveresk and Mrs. Carlyle, [n.pub], [n.d]. Letter 31.

7. George Castle's Trafalgar Letter, *The Nelson Dispatch*, Vol. 6, Part 8, (October 1998), p. 346. A copy of the letter appears in the appendix.

8. *Newcastle Courant*, 23 November 1805.

9. Clayton, T. & Craig, P., *Trafalgar: The Men, The Battle, The Storm*, Hodder & Stoughton (2004), p. 316.

10. The National Archives (TNA), ADM 51/1739. Log of the *Scout*, 9-11 and 20 July 1807.

11. Log of the *Scout*, 14 July 1807.

12. Log of the *Scout*, 2 November 1807.

13. Pocock, T., *Remember Nelson; The Life of Captain Sir William Hoste*. Collins (1977), p. 138.

14. Brett-James, A., (ed.) *Escape from the French: Captain Hewson's Narrative 1803-1809*, Webb & Bower (1981), p. 165. For an account of the escape from Lt. O'Brien's perspective see also Adkins, R. & L. *The War of All the Oceans*, Abacus (2006), pp. 241-250.

15. *London Gazette*, Issue number 16320, 28 November–2 December 1809, pp. 1906-1907. www.london-gazette.co.uk [Accessed 21 April 2009].

16. Pocock, *Remember Nelson: The Life of Captain William Hoste*, pp. 149-151.

17. Hughes, *Private Correspondence of Admiral Lord Collingwood*, Admiral Collingwood to his sister, 13 August 1809.

18. TNA, ADM 51/1929, Log of the *Scout*, 28 July 1809.

19. Hughes, *Private Correspondence*, Admiral Collingwood to his sister, 25 November 1809.

20. Adams, M., *Admiral Collingwood*, Weidenfeld & Nicholson (2005), pp. 271-273.

21. TNA, ADM 37/3092. Muster Book of the *Kingfisher*.

22. TNA, ADM 51/2495. Log of the *Kingfisher*, 7 October 1811.

23. *London Gazette*, Issue number 16586, 24 March 1812, pp. 563-64. Codrington's despatch named the captured lieutenant as Lt. Cattle, but it seems likely that this was a spelling error and should be Lt. Castle. www.london-gazette.co.uk [Accessed 21 April 2009].

24. *London Gazette*, Issue number 16668, 7-14 November 1812, pp. 2295-2296. www.london-gazette.co.uk [Accessed 21 April 2009].

25. *Formidable* had been part of the van division of the Combined Fleet at Trafalgar but was captured off Ferrol by Admiral Strachan's squadron in November 1805.

26. James, W., *Naval History of Great Britain*, (1826) Vol.V, pp. 356-7.

27. *London Gazette*, Issue number 17062, 18 September 1815, pp. 1909-1914. www.london-gazette.co.uk [Accessed 21 April 2009].

28. TNA, ADM 51/2494. Log of the *Larne*, 11 March – 18 April 1817.

29. Pope, D., *Life in Nelson's Navy*, Chatham Publishing (1997), p. 138.

30. Pope, D., pp. 140-41.

31. Log of the *Larne*, 26 September 1817.

32. Log of the *Larne*, 24 October 1817.

33. *Newcastle Courant*, 10 January 1818.

34. Inscription on a headstone in the parish church of St. Mary le Bow, Durham.

35. TNA, C211/31/3, Commissions and Inquisitions of Lunacy and burial register of St. John the Baptist, Dinsdale, 15 April 1865.

36. Rodger, N.A.M., Commissioned officers' careers in the Royal Navy, 1690-1815, *Journal of Maritime History*, (June 2001).

37. Greenhill, B. & Gifford, A., *Steam, Politics and Patronage: The Transformation of the Royal Navy, 1815-54*, Conway Maritime Press (1994), p. 75.

38. Greenhill & Gifford, p. 61.

39. Perhaps the best known, contemporary representative of this Northumbrian naval tradition is Admiral Sir Nigel Essenhigh (1944-). He became the captain of the aircraft carrier *H.M.S. Ark Royal* when she was first commissioned in 1985 and subsequently served as First Sea Lord in 2001 before his retirement. Admiral Essenhigh, like Collingwood, was born in Newcastle.

Appendix

George Castle's Trafalgar Letter

H.M.S. Royal Sovereign
Gibraltar
3 November 1805

Dear Sister,

By the great Mercy of God I am left safe and unhurt both from the Enemy and the Elements, for I can safely say we have engaged both. But thank God our poor shattered ship has arrived here this evening after tossing about more than a week at the mercy of wind and waves. I shall proceed to give as much account as I can of the Glorious 21st of October – that was truly a glorious day for us. But stop! In gaining a battle we have lost a brave Commander, he fell gloriously just as a Briton ought to die – he has done his duty to his Country and has gone to rest where neither war nor slaughter reach and has left room for others to follow his example, we will let our Enemies see though they have deprived us of one Nelson, we have more in store.

On 19th of October the lookout ships made the signal the enemy was put to sea but in the evening they put in again. We saw them to leeward of us again on Sunday the 20th it was then very bad weather, and they were close to the land, so that we could not bear down upon them by reason of a lee shore. However on the next morning by daylight we saw them further from the land, we immediately bore up for them. We led the Van, ran right down among them, this ship sails very well indeed, she was 55 minutes engaged with them before any other ship came to our assistance and we were alongside a great three-decker. I can assure you it was glorious work, I think you would like to have seen me thump into her quarter. I am stationed at the heaviest gun in the ship and I stuck so close to one gun and poured it into her, she was so close it was impossible to miss her. She behaved very rascally for when she first struck to us, she went round our bows and when right ahead of us up with her ensign and raked us but we soon brought our starboard guns to bear upon her, crash went her masts and then she was fairly sicken'd – she was a Spanish Admiral's ship but the Admiral was killed and after that we made an 84 strike to us. I looked once out of our stern ports – but I saw nothing but French and Spaniards round firing at us in all directions – it was shocking to see many brave seamen mangled so, some with their heads half shot away, others with their entrails mashed lying panting upon the deck. The greatest slaughter was upon the quarterdeck and the Poop – we had seven ships upon us at once – the *Belleisle* was next to us in the Action and she kept off a great deal of fire from us, likewise the *Tonnant*. We began the engagement a quarter before twelve and did not cease firing until three in the afternoon but we had not ended entirely till sunset when remnants of the enemy's fleet went away to Cadiz.

We have got 200 prisoners on board, French and Spaniards, they are droll looking fellows, they say they took us for the *Victory* and were determined to sink us, but I believe they found it hard work to sink a British Man of War.

N.B. This copy of Castle's letter was published in *The Nelson Dispatch*, Vol. 6, Part 8, (October 1998) p. 346. The original letter was the property of a Miss Robinson of Alton in Staffordshire. Castle was the great uncle of the lady to whose grandmother the letter was written. George Castle had six sisters. It is assumed that two of them, Eleanor (b.1797) and Francis Susanna (b.1801), were too young to correspond with their brother as early as 1805, whereas Hannah (b.1793) and Martha (b.1796) were unmarried and childless. It is likely therefore that the letter was written either to his eldest sister Sarah (b. 1782) or to Ann (b.1792).

Bibliography

A note about primary sources

Much of the detail about the careers of Collingwood's Northumbrians is derived from a range of primary sources held in the collections of The National Archives, Kew; National Maritime Museum, Greenwich; the British Library; and Northumberland Record Office. Readers inclined to pursue their own research of naval topics or wish to recover detail about an ancestor who served in the Royal Navy during Collingwood's era will find a good deal of relevant information in the archives of these institutions. As with most books of this kind considerably more sources were consulted than those specifically cited in the text and referenced in the endnotes. What follows, therefore, represents a selection of the primary sources that might be of particular interest to family historians and those interested in aspects of naval history. The best starting point for genealogists is *The National Archives Readers Guide, Tracing your Naval Ancestors* (2003) by Bruno Pappalardo. For those interested in more general subjects like naval administration, conditions of service, fleet actions or the careers of particular ships, a *Guide to Naval Records in The National Archives of the UK* (2006) edited by R. Cock and N.A.M. Rodger is advised. Each of the four institutions has an extensive, user-friendly website providing researchers with helpful advice, user guides and facilities to search catalogues. Readers are encouraged to visit these websites at an early stage.

The National Archives: www.nationalarchives.gov.uk

ADM 1

Admiralty, and Ministry of Defence, Navy Department: Correspondence and Papers, 1660-1976

The Original Series (first group) contains both admirals' and captains' in-letters. The latter are arranged chronologically and alphabetically by initial letter of the captain's surname. They record numerous aspects of the exchange of information between the Admiralty and individual captains in relation to administrative duties, orders, matters of discipline, accidents and naval actions. Courts Martial Evidence and Papers are also contained within the ADM 1 collection and helpful indexes can be found in ADM 12 & 13.

ADM 9

Admiralty: Survey Returns of Officers' Services, 1817-1848

Beginning in 1817 the Admiralty obliged naval officers to submit a form providing information about their naval service. The entries summarise the ranks they held, ships served in with dates, flag officers, captains and commanders served under and the principal stations on which the ships were employed, including any fleet actions they were involved in. This basic information enables researchers to identify other relevant sources within the ADM collections such as Muster Books (ADM 36 & 37) and captains' logs (ADM 51 & 52).

There is an index to the collection in ADM 10. Other useful sources for the service records of individual officers can be found in ADM 6 – Lieutenant's Passing Certificates and ADM 11 – Succession Books of Commissioned and Standing Officers – although both can be rather more time consuming to research.

ADM 36 & 37

Admiralty: Royal Navy Ships' Muster Books 1688-1842

Ships' muster books are a basic source for genealogists but can only be used if the name of the ship and the dates of an individual's service on board it are already known. Indexes to the names of ships and the periods covered by their muster books are available on the open shelves and must be consulted first to provide a reference to the piece number of a particular book. For example, the full reference to the muster book of *Royal Sovereign* for October 1805 is ADM 36/15754. Once located, the muster books provide information about the name, age, rank and place of abode of individual officers and seamen, the date of their first appearance on board, period of service and reason for discharge.

ADM 51 & 53

Admiralty: Captains' Logs (1669-1853) and Ships' Logs (1799-1985)

Keeping a daily logbook was, and still is, a fundamental part of the management of a ship at sea. Most of the information recorded, especially for the logbooks in the ADM 53 collection, relates to weather conditions, wind strength and direction, observed latitudes at noon, courses steered, sail changes and ships spoken. Logbooks in the ADM 51 collection, however, are more like journals and record information about discipline, punishment (usually floggings), actions with enemy vessels, deaths on board and other incidents. Such information helps to provide a detailed context in which to understand the experience of individual officers and men.

In addition to these primary sources there are numerous secondary and contemporary printed sources on the open shelves at the National Archives which help researchers to locate specific records or provide contextual information. Those of most use to genealogists are: *Steel's Original and Correct List of the Royal Navy*, published annually from 1782-1814, relevant volumes published by the *List and Index Society and Commissioned Sea Officers of the Royal Navy 1660-1815*, Prof. D. Syrett and Dr. R.L. Dinardo (Eds.), published by the Navy Records Society whose website: www.navyrecords.org.uk is also worth a visit.

National Maritime Museum: www.nmm.ac.uk

The collections of the National Maritime Museum are almost as extensive as those of the National Archives. They can be consulted by arrangement with the Caird Library which administers access to original documents and a comprehensive collection of reference books. The particular collections used for *Collingwood's Northumbrians* were the correspondence and papers of Admiral Robert Roddam, together with the Letter Books and so-called Commonplace Book of Captain Edward Rotheram. Admiral Roddam's papers were deposited with the museum by the Holderness-Roddam family in 1967 and 1973. The archive includes logbooks, letter books, official correspondence, orders and miscellaneous papers which collectively represent one of the most comprehensive sets of records available to study the career of an eighteenth century admiral. The Rotheram collection is much smaller by comparison and rather more eclectic. Nevertheless, it is extensively used by maritime historians of the Napoleonic period. Individual items within these collections can be identified online by accessing: www.nmm.ac.uk/collections/archive/catalogue

The British Library: www.bl.uk

Despite the size and comprehensive nature of the collections held by the British Library, research was limited to aspects of its East India Company archive. Specifically, the logbooks and journals of *Thetis* for her voyages to India and China between 1786 and 1796 when Collingwood's lieutenant, William Landless, was serving as a marine officer.

Northumberland Record Office: www.northumberland.gov.uk

Northumberland Record Office at Woodhorn hold numerous collections of family papers that offer insights into many aspects of the economic, social and political character of the county during the eighteenth and early nineteenth centuries. Those of particular significance for the research of *Collingwood's Northumbrians* were the Blackett and Delaval collections.

Admiral Collingwood corresponded regularly with his father-in-law, John Erasmus Blackett, and seven letters, written between 1794 and 1801, survive under reference NRO ZBL 247. They offer information about Collingwood's opinions and attitudes to politics, the state of the Navy before the Great Mutinies of 1797 as well as a graphic account of the battle of Cape St. Vincent. A further six letters exchanged between Blackett and other correspondents, listed under reference NRO ZBE 228 and dated between 1789 and 1803, offer naval historians some interesting case studies of the workings of naval patronage.

The Delaval papers represent one of the largest family collections held by Northumberland Record Office. Several members of the family rose to high positions in the Royal Navy, notably Sir Ralph and Sir George Delaval who both became admirals between 1690 and 1720. Some of their naval papers survive under reference NRO 1 DE/1, 6 and 12 and there are some further supplementary papers in NRO 650.

During the second half of the eighteenth century, Sir John Hussey Delaval, together with his brother Thomas, invested considerable sums of money in the development of industrial enterprise at Seaton Sluice and agricultural improvement on their estates at Ford. As MP for Berwick, Sir John received numerous requests to use his influence to secure employment or preferment for his supporters. Within the collection, listed under reference NRO 2 DE 45, there are over a hundred letters, many of them exchanged between Sir John and his election agent at Berwick, Lieutenant George

Younghusband, and other members of his family. They offer maritime historians a useful case study of the workings of naval patronage, as well as its limitations, during the reign of George III.

Other naval records consulted at Woodhorn include some miscellaneous correspondence of Admiral Roddam, and a copy of his will, under the references NRO 329/1-8 and NRO 5935/10.

Secondary sources

Newspapers

Newcastle Courant

Durham County Advertiser

London Gazette: www.london-gazette.co.uk

Books

Adams, M., *Admiral Collingwood: Nelson's Own Hero*. Weidenfeld & Nicholson (2005).

Adkins, R., *Trafalgar: The Biography of a Battle*. Abacus (2004).

Adkins, R. & L., *The War for All the Oceans*. Abacus (2007).

Barrow, T., *Trafalgar Geordies and North Country Seamen of Nelson's Navy, 1793-1815*. North East England Press (2005).

Black, J. & Woodfine, P. (eds.), *The British Navy and the use of Naval Power in the Eighteenth Century*. Leicester University Press (1988).

Brenchley, D., *A Place by Itself – Berwick-upon-Tweed in the Eighteenth Century*. Berwick-upon-Tweed Civic Society (1997).

Brenchley, D., Beith, A., et.al., *Berwick in Parliament*. Berwick-upon-Tweed History Society (2001).

Clayton, T., *Tars: The Men who made Britain Rule the Waves*. Hodder & Stoughton (2007).

Clayton, T. & Craig P., *Trafalgar: the Men, the Battle, the Storm.* Hodder & Stoughton (2004).

Colledge, J.J. & Warlow, B., *Ships of the Royal Navy.* Chatham Publishing (2006).

Cordingly, D., *Billy Ruffian: The Bellerophon and the Downfall of Napoleon.* Bloomsbury Publishing (2004).

Duffy, M. & Morriss, R. (eds.), *The Glorious First of June 1794: A Naval Battle and its Aftermath.* University of Exeter Press (2001).

Duffy, M. (ed.), *Naval Miscellany*, Vol. VI. Ashgate for Navy Records Society (2003).

Gardiner, R., *Navies in the American Revolution.* Chatham Publishing (1996).

Greenhill, B. & Gifford, A., *Steam, Politics and Patronage: The Transformation of the Royal Navy, 1815-54.* Conway Maritime Press (1994).

Hall, C.D., *Wellington's Navy: Sea Power and the Peninsular War, 1807-1814.* Chatham Publishing (2004).

Harding, R. (ed.), *A Great and Glorious Victory: New Perspectives on the Battle of Trafalgar.* Seaforth Publishing (2008).

Heathcote, T.A., *Nelson's Trafalgar Captains and their Battles.* Pen and Sword Maritime (2005).

Hughes, E., *North Country Life in the Eighteenth Century, Vol. I: The North East 1700-1750.* Oxford University Press (1952).

Hughes, E., *The Private Correspondence of Admiral Lord Collingwood.* Navy Records Society (1957).

Langford, P., *A Polite and Commercial People: England, 1727-1783.* Oxford University Press (1989).

Lavery, B., *Nelson's Fleet at Trafalgar.* National Maritime Museum (2004).

Lavery, B., *Nelson's Navy: The Ships, Men and Organisation, 1793-1815.* Conway Maritime Press (1989).

Lewis, M., *A Social History of the Navy, 1793-1815.* Allen & Unwin (1960).

McCord, N., *North East England: The Region's Development 1760-1960*. Batsford (1979).

McCord, N. & Purdue B., *British History, 1815-1914*. Oxford University Press (2007).

Murray, G., *Life of Admiral Collingwood*. Hutchinson & Co. (1936).

Newnham Collingwood, G.L., *A Selection from the Public and Private Correspondence of Vice-Admiral Lord Collingwood*. James Ridgeway (1829).

Orde, D., *Nelson's Mediterranean Command*. The Pentland Press (1997).

Orde, D., *The Life of Admiral Lord Collingwood*. Pen and Sword Publications (2008).

Pocock, T., *Remember Nelson: The Life of Captain William Hoste*. Collins (1977).

Pocock, T., *Battle for Empire*. Caxton Editions (2002).

Pope, D., *Life in Nelson's Navy*. Chatham Publishing (1997).

Purdue, A.W., *Merchants and Gentry in North East England, 1650-1830. The Carrs and the Ellisons*. University of Sunderland Press (1999).

Purdue, A.W., *The Ship that Came Home: The Story of a Northern Dynasty*. Third Millennium Publishing (2004).

Rodger, N.A.M., *The Wooden World: An Anatomy of the Georgian Navy*. Collins (1986).

Rodger, N.A.M., *The Command of the Ocean*. Penguin Books (2004).

Spinney, D., *Rodney*. Allen & Unwin (1969).

Sutton, J., *Lords of the East: The East India Company and its Ships, 1600-1874*. Conway Maritime Press (2000).

Tracey, N., *Who's Who in Nelson's Navy*. Chatham Publishing (2006).

Tracey, N. (ed.), *The Naval Chronicle,* Vol. V (1807-1810) and Vol. V (1811-1815). Chatham Publishing (1999).

Warner, O., *The Glorious First of June*. Batsford (1961).

Essays and articles

Breen, K., Graves and Hood at the Chesapeake. *Mariner's Mirror*, 66, 1, (1980), pp. 53-65.

Johnson, G., Our Visit to Holy Island in May 1854. *History of the Berwickshire Naturalists' Club*, Vol. 7 (1873-75), p. 40.

Rodger, N.A.M., Shipboard Life in the Georgian Navy, 1750-1800: The Decline of the Old Order? *The North Sea: Twelve Essays on the Social History of Maritime Labour.* Fischer, L.R., Hamre, H., Holm, P. & Bruijn, J.R. (eds.), Stavanger Maritime Museum, (1992), pp. 29-39.

Rodger, N.A.M., A Little Navy of Your Own Making. Admiral Boscawen and the Cornish Connection in the Royal Navy. *Parameters of British Naval Power, 1650-1850.* Duffy, M. (ed.) University of Exeter Press (1992), pp. 82-92.

Rodger, N.A.M., Commissioned officers' careers in the Royal Navy, 1690-1815, *Journal for Maritime Research*, June 2001. Accessed online at: www.jmr.nmm.ac.uk

Rodger, N.A.M., Honour and Duty at Sea, 1660-1815, *Bulletin of the Institute of Historical Research*, Vol. 75, no. 190, (2002).

Speck, W.A., Northumberland Elections in the Eighteenth Century, *Northern History*, Vol. XXVIII (1992), pp. 164-177.

Spinney, D., Rodney and the Saintes: A Reassessment, *Mariner's Mirror*, 68, 4, (1982), pp. 377-389.

Staniforth, F., Collingwood's Captain – Two Letters. *Archaeologia Aeliana (4th Series) Vol. XLIII* (1965) pp. 306-314.

Staniforth, F., Admiral Collingwood and his flag-captain on the *Royal Sovereign*, Edward Rotheram, *North Magazine*, Vol. 4 (1971), pp. 14-15.

Index

Index of ships

British warships

A

Achille [74], 61
Adventure [12], 15
Agamemnon [64], 1
Alarm [4], 15
Alfred [74], 82-83
Amphion [32], 106-108
Andromache [32], 50

B

Badger [14], 19
Barfleur [98], 19, 22, 49-50, 52, 83
Belle Poule [38], 110
Belleisle [74], 64, 104
Bellerophon [74], 48, 57, 64-70
Blake [74], 111-112
Bombay Castle [74], 51
Brave [80], 112
Bristol [50], 33
Brunswick [74], 53, 114
Bulldog, 117

C

Camel (Storeship), 54
Camilla [20], 55
Carcass [8], 88
Centaur [74], 49, 83
Childers [18], 112

Colchester [60], 34
Colossus [74], 61, 110
Conquestador [60], 79
Convert [32], 82
Cornwall [74], 37-38
Culloden [74], 48, 52-54

D

Defence [74], 52
Dreadnought [60], 33
Dreadnought [98], 21, 47, 59-61,
67, 78, 91-93, 103

E

Espiegle [18], 112-113
Euryalus [36], 63, 112
Excellent [74], 22, 102

F

Flora [36], 50
Franchise [36], 111

G

Glenmore [36], 87
Grasshopper [18], 105-106
Greenwich [50], 33-34
Greyhound [24], 30-32

H

Hawke [16], 55-56
Hector [44], 32
Hector [74], 83
Hermes [20], 112-113
Hinchinbrooke [28], 19
Hussar [38], 35
Hydra [38], 41

French and Spanish warships

Merchant ships and prizes